FAMILY LIFE IN SHAKESPEARE'S ENGLAND

STRATFORD-UPON-AVON
1570–1630

Publications of
The Shakespeare Birthplace Trust
in association with
Sutton Publishing Limited

Robert Bearman
Shakespeare in the Stratford Records
1994

Joan Lane
John Hall and his Patients:
The Medical Practice of Shakespeare's Son-in-Law
1996

Philip Tennant
The Civil War in Stratford-upon-Avon:
Conflict and Community in South Warwickshire 1642–1646
1996

FAMILY LIFE IN SHAKESPEARE'S ENGLAND

STRATFORD-UPON-AVON 1570–1630

JEANNE JONES

SUTTON PUBLISHING

THE SHAKESPEARE BIRTHPLACE TRUST

First published in 1996 by
Sutton Publishing Limited · Phoenix Mill
Thrupp · Stroud · Gloucestershire · GL5 2BU
in association with
The Shakespeare Birthplace Trust
The Shakespeare Centre · Henley Street · Stratford-upon-Avon

Reprinted 1998

Copyright © Jeanne Jones, 1996

British Library Cataloguing in Publication Data
A catalogue record for this book is available from the British Library

ISBN 0-7509-1261-8

Cover picture: A Family Saying Grace before a Meal *by Anthonius Claeissins (c. 1538–1613) (Shakespeare Birthplace Trust Collection)*

 ALAN SUTTON™ and SUTTON™ are the
trade marks of Sutton Publishing Limited

Typeset in 12/16 Garamond.
Typesetting and origination by
Sutton Publishing Limited.
Printed in Great Britain by
WBC Limited, Bridgend.

CONTENTS

General Editors' Preface

The objects of The Shakespeare Birthplace Trust, as defined by the Act of Parliament under which it operates, are:

a) to promote in every part of the world the appreciation and study of the plays and other works of William Shakespeare and the general advancement of Shakespearian knowledge;

b) to maintain and preserve the Shakespeare birthplace properties for the benefit of the nation;

c) to provide and maintain for the benefit of the nation a museum and a library of books, manuscripts, records of historic interest, pictures, photographs and objects of antiquity with particular but not exclusive reference to William Shakespeare, his life, works and times.

It is from these objectives that the series of publications, of which this volume is part, derives. The central focus of the series is Shakespeare: his plays and their performance, his life, and the environment, historical, topographical, and domestic, in which he lived; and the raw material for volumes in the series is derived largely from the rich Shakespearian holdings of the Trust's Library and Records Office, in the form of printed books and archival and pictorial material relating to Shakespeare's life in Stratford, to the history of the town, to scholarship and criticism on his writings, and to the performance history of his plays. Such a collection of volumes, covering a wide range of topics – theatrical, literary and historical – cannot, of course, observe rigid editorial uniformity. To a considerable extent, therefore, treatment and approach from volume to volume are determined by the aims and needs of individual authors and editors. Within this rather broad scope, however, we seek to produce a series of volumes that will be of interest to the general reader while maintaining a high standard of scholarship in the furtherance of that basic objective of the Shakespeare Birthplace Trust, the general advancement of Shakespearian knowledge.

Robert Bearman
Robert Smallwood

LIST OF ILLUSTRATIONS

The furniture and household items illustrated in this study are all from the collections of the Shakespeare Birthplace Trust.

LIST OF FIGURES AND TABLES

Figure

ACKNOWLEDGEMENTS

I have received help from many people while writing this book. Particular thanks are due to Mairi Macdonald and all the staff of the Shakespeare Birthplace Trust Record Office, to Mrs Marian Pringle, Dr Susan Brock, and Dr Pat Hughes. But my greatest debt is to Dr Robert Bearman and Dr Robert Smallwood for their always welcome advice and their unfailing encouragement.

Jeanne Jones
Stratford-upon-Avon, 1996

AUTHOR'S NOTE

Unless otherwise stated, the originals of the inventories and wills referred to in this book are held at the Shakespeare Birthplace Trust Record Office in Stratford-upon-Avon, or at the Hereford and Worcester County Record Office with photocopies at Stratford. References have been given only for those wills held at the Hereford and Worcester County Record Office, photocopies of which are not held at Stratford, and for those wills held at the Public Record Office, London.

A glossary of archaic words used in the wills and inventories will be found after the Appendix.

INTRODUCTION

As you drive into Warwickshire today, a notice by the road informs you that this is 'Shakespeare's County'. How surprised the Shakespeare family and their contemporaries would have been. To be sure, Shakespeare became a wealthy man by Stratford standards, and bought one of the most imposing houses in the small market town. Leading members of the community called on him when they wished to borrow money. But on the inhabitants of the borough and those who lived in the outlying hamlets which made up the parish of Stratford, William's activities had little effect. His father, John, had, for a while, been one of the ruling oligarchy of aldermen and capital burgesses who, together with the ecclesiastical authorities, endeavoured to bring order into the townsmen's lives, but, by the turn of the century, he had fallen on lean times and had resigned from the Corporation – and he had never had the same impact on the life of the town as had such as Adrian Quiney and his son, Richard, or as Master Daniel Baker.

This study will be about the ordinary people of Stratford, most of whom, unlike Shakespeare, spent their whole lives in the town or its immediate environs. It will range from the wealthy innkeepers and merchants to the humble labourers and almsfolk. These last may well have been included among the 700 poor folk to whom the bailiff and burgesses referred in a petition of 1601 as living within the town.[1] But the desperately poor left little in the way of documentary evidence to help us learn more of their lives, and consequently will figure in this study only when seen through the eyes of their more fortunate contemporaries – in the church registers, court records or Corporation minutes.

For the rest, the starting point has been the collection of sixteenth-

and seventeenth-century wills and inventories held, for the most part, at the Shakespeare Birthplace Trust Record Office in Stratford. Others are held at Hereford and Worcester County Record Office, for Stratford was then in the diocese of Worcester; and some wills, those of persons who owned property in more than one diocese, are held at the Public Record Office in London. Although, among the whole sample, the earliest wills are dated 1500 and the later wills and inventories continue well past the end of the seventeenth century, it has been necessary, in order to keep this work within manageable proportions, to limit the number of inventories used to those made between 1570 and 1630. These are the inventories of people whom Shakespeare may well have seen and recognized from the age of six until his death. Very occasionally, to illustrate a particular point, an inventory or will made outside these parameters will be referred to, but the names mentioned therein will not necessarily be included among those on whom this study is based.

When wills were proved in the ecclesiastical court, they had to be accompanied by an inventory of all the testator's goods. Although in many cases both will and inventory remained together, in other cases they have become separated over the years and only the will or the inventory has survived. It is, therefore, impossible to calculate what proportion of the population made wills, but, since the extant ones include those of people who owned less than a pound's worth of goods, it is clear that will-making was not confined to the wealthier townsfolk. The inventories, 168 in all, have been transcribed, and notes have been taken of the 157 wills. The names of the appraisers and witnesses of the inventories, and the legatees, executors, overseers, debtors, creditors and witnesses of the wills were noted, and other documents, such as leases, court records, letters, registers of baptisms, burials and marriages, Corporation minutes and chamberlains' accounts, were then consulted. The names of any persons who clearly lived outside the parish were discarded. This resulted in a cohort of

800 persons living in Stratford and its surrounding hamlets, between 1570 and 1630, about whom several facts were known. These are the people who figure in this study.

The earliest known map of Stratford is that of Samuel Winter dated 1759, but the layout of the town had not altered since it was founded by the then Bishop of Worcester in 1196 and, indeed, the gridiron pattern of its streets remains virtually intact today. Prior to 1553 the town came under the jurisdiction of the lord of the manor to whom the ground rent was paid and who dispensed justice. Until 1547, when it was dissolved, the Gild of the Holy Cross was a potent force in the town. Although its primary concern was the salvation of the souls of its members, the gild also dispensed charity, and was responsible for the twenty-four almshouses, the free school, the gild hall and chapel, and the fine bridge over the Avon. It drew its members from all classes of society and from a wide area, who paid what they could afford in money, goods or services, receiving in return the assurance that they would be remembered in prayer after death. Many of the wealthier members left property to the gild in their wills. The officers were town worthies and among their more agreeable tasks was the organization of feasts and pageants.

Small wonder, then, that the gild was sorely missed at its dissolution. In 1553, six days before his death, the young Edward VI granted the town's petition for a charter, no doubt prompted by his uncle, the Duke of Northumberland, lord of the manor of Stratford. The charter named fourteen townsmen, most of whom had been officers of the gild, to be aldermen, and from their number they were to elect yearly a bailiff (mayor) and a chief alderman. Fourteen capital burgesses were to be chosen by the company and these twenty-eight men were to form the town council. They were to be responsible for the bridge, almshouses, school and chapel and the town was granted the gild properties which became the source of most of its income. Permission was granted for the continuation of the weekly market and two annual fairs. The borough was to be responsible for the salaries of the vicar and schoolmaster, although their appointments had to be ratified by the lord of the manor who also expected to be consulted about the choice of bailiff. Neither he nor the lord-lieutenant of the county had any jurisdiction over law and order in the town where the bailiff and chief alderman were also justices of the peace.

In the first two decades covered by this book there seems to have been little friction between the town and the lord of the manor, Ambrose Dudley, Earl of Warwick. However, on his death in 1590, the lordship was granted to Sir Edward Greville of nearby Milcote and there were differences of opinion both with him and his successor, Lionel Cranfield, Earl of Middlesex, mainly with regard to the choices of bailiff and vicar. A further charter, granted in 1610, went a little way towards clarifying the situation but some antagonism remained.

Besides being a borough and a manor, the town was also part of a parish. The collegiate church of the Holy Trinity stood outside the borough in Old Stratford and the vicar had the cure of the several hundred inhabitants who lived in the outlying hamlets of Bridgetown, Welcombe, Luddington, Drayton, Clopton, Ryne Clifford, Dodwell, Bishopton and Shottery as well as of the inhabitants of the borough itself, the population of which has been calculated as being 2,200 in 1595.[2]

Shortly after its incorporation the borough had been faced with two epidemics which caused a steep decline in its population. In 1558, 145 people were buried during what seems to have been an outbreak of influenza or, possibly, typhus. According to Alan Dyer this was over 10 per cent of the population.[3] The plague year of 1564 saw another 254 burials, although the average yearly burial rate between these dates had been thirty-eight. Over the next thirty years the number of baptisms exceeded the number of burials by 341 in spite of another outbreak of plague in 1587; together with immigration from the surrounding countryside, this resulted in a rise in the population.

In the mid-1590s the town had to deal with further crises. There were two disastrous fires in 1594 and 1595. In a petition of 1598 the bailiff and burgesses reported that 200 dwelling houses and £12,000 worth of household goods were destroyed.[4] It is as well, however, to remember that, as it was a petition, some exaggeration may have been involved. Although, apparently, no lives were lost, the temporary lack of housing discouraged further immigration. In 1597 the whole country suffered from dearth due to disastrous harvests and this meant that malnutrition took its toll of the population, with 313 burials in Stratford in three years. Valiant efforts to rebuild both population and houses were hampered by further outbreaks of plague in the mid-1610s, another fire in 1614 and dearth once again in the 1620s.

The question arises: did these epidemics and fires affect the economy of the town, causing its permanent decline, or were they short-term crises which were subsequently overcome?[5] Although it is now twenty years since the debate as to the decline or otherwise of sixteenth-century towns was at its height, the question still exercises the minds of local historians. A study of the finances of individuals, as well as of the Corporation, should help to decide where Stratford stands in this debate.

Stratford-upon-Avon numbered among its inhabitants yeomen and farm labourers, craftsmen and traders, gentlemen of leisure and those who aspired to gentility. There were merchants with well-furnished houses and poor people who owned little or nothing. There were zealous puritans and those who resented them, recusants, almsfolk, orphans, vagrants and felons. The people of this town, which lies in the very heart of England, represent in microcosm the ordinary people who lived in the towns and villages throughout the country. This book, therefore, while aiming to place in perspective the position of the Shakespeares in sixteenth- and early seventeenth-century Stratford and, at the same time, tracing the fortunes of the town, will also reflect the lives and attitudes of Shakespeare's contemporaries throughout England.

Lewis Hiccox's tavern (Shakespeare's Birthplace) furnished according to his inventory of 1627 (see page 50).

The ground and first floors of the front range viewed from the street.

The attics and rear wing viewed from the garden.

PAT HUGHES '96

CHAPTER ONE

WHERE THEY LIVED

When the town of Stratford-upon-Avon was laid out in 1196, it was on a site adjoining a village which had existed since Saxon times. The area of the new borough was 109 acres and it was designed to take about 400 houses and shops along the roads set roughly in a gridiron pattern. These were divided into burgages 3½ perches by 12 perches (52 ft by 198 ft) for which a yearly rent of 12*d* was paid to the bishop as lord of the manor. Over the years these burgages were divided up or amalgamated so that, by the sixteenth century, some house owners were paying 3*d* chief rent for a quarter of a burgage, while some others paid 3*s* 6*d* for three and a half burgages.

In the sixteenth and seventeenth centuries the seventeen streets and lanes of the borough were divided into six wards for administrative purposes. Each ward was named after its principal street and was presided over by two headboroughs, leading townsmen who lived within the ward. Bridge Street ward extended from the bridge to the market cross and included the row of houses and shops which ran along the middle, called, appropriately enough, Middle Row. This divided Fore Bridge Street on the south from Back Bridge Street on the north. The gardens of the houses in Back Bridge Street ran down to Gilpits, an open watercourse, which probably also served as a sewer and general rubbish dump. High Street ward consisted of just the one street, running southwards at right angles to Bridge Street. Chapel Street, a continuation of High Street, gave its name to the ward which also contained Church Street and Chapel Lane. Sheep Street ward also covered Waterside or Bancroftside. Wood Street ward contained most of the streets lying to the west of High Street and Chapel Street – Greenhill Street, Rother Market, Ely Street (or Swine Street) and Tinkers' Lane (now Scholars' Lane). The sixth was Henley Street ward,

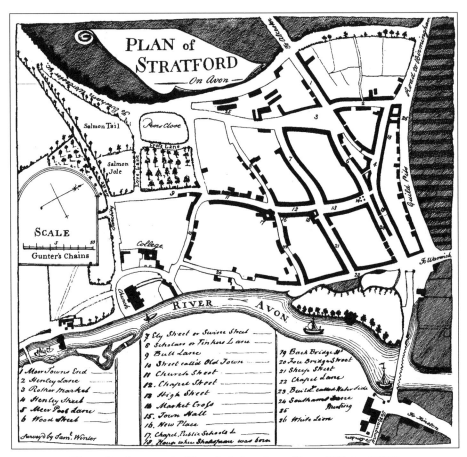

The earliest known map of Stratford-upon-Avon. (Samuel Winter, 1759)

made up of the street which led towards Henley-in-Arden, and also
Wynsor (now Windsor Street) and Mere Street. Like the gardens in
Back Bridge Street, those on the north side of Henley Street ran down
to the Gilpits.

Each ward and, indeed, each street had its own particular features.
Bridge Street was the first street a traveller from the south would enter
on crossing Clopton Bridge and, therefore, it is not surprising that it
contained four inns. The two largest, the Swan and the Bear, stood

opposite each other at the river end. The other two, the Crown in Fore Bridge Street and the Angel at the west end of Back Bridge Street, were owned by the Corporation and each leased out at an annual rent of 33s 4d.

Although, in some cases, dwelling houses contained rooms which were used as shops or had a lean-to at the side or front for trading, Middle Row was made up of shops which were built especially for that purpose with dwelling places above and between them. Between 1570 and 1630 five bakers plied their trade in this ward, although never more than two at any one time. Otherwise it seems to have been the focus of the leather trade as four shoemakers as well as a glover, a tanner and two saddlers lived and worked there. Hides for the leather were, no doubt, supplied by one of the five butchers trading in the ward. Over the sixty years, sons followed fathers into both their trades and their premises.

Three butchers also traded in High Street, one renting the tenement which was also used as the gaol, and another, a house called 'The Cage' which stood at the corner of Bridge Street. The third, Thomas Rogers, yeoman, butcher and corndealer, built the house, which still stands, known as Harvard House, so-called because his daughter married into the Harvard family and became the mother of the founder of the university. The properties which the Corporation owned in High Street were let at the highest rents in Stratford and the street was clearly considered a desirable place for trading since two mercers and two woollen drapers, all wealthy by Stratford standards, traded there, three of them from their dwelling houses, and the fourth, John Brown, from a shop in a house known as Beason's House, although he lived in Sheep Street.

Chapel Street, running from Sheep Street to Chapel Lane, contained the houses of wealthy yeomen and gentlemen. Shakespeare's New Place stood there, next to the property later owned by Thomas Nash, who married Shakespeare's granddaughter Elizabeth. The Reynolds family lived in a house which is now the northern end of the Shakespeare Hotel. The vicar's house was in Church Street which also contained the twenty-four almshouses, by the side of the free school and the gild chapel. Rooms over the almshouses and in the chapel yard were let at low rents. Chapel Lane (or Dead Lane) runs down towards the river between Chapel Street and Church Street and contained several barns, although there were also some cottages, for in John Brown's inventory we can read of 'one other lease ther of certayne tenementes wherein pore people do dwell . . . vi^{s}viii^d'. Workers in the cloth trade congregated, appropriately enough, in or close to Sheep Street. Six woollen drapers lived there during the sixty years as well as two fullers and four weavers. During the period under review, the barns in Waterside were gradually being converted into dwelling houses.

Not all the wealthier townsfolk lived in Chapel Street ward. We find them also in the other wards although not in quite such close proximity to one another. The large property which Francis Smith of Wootton Wawen leased to Richard Hill, woollen draper, stood in Wood Street, at its corner with the High Street. The site covered three and a half burgages (approximately 36,000 sq. ft). The house was damaged by fire in 1594 and was rebuilt by Hill's son-in-law, Abraham Sturley, who had taken over the lease after Hill's death, although Katharine Hill, Richard's widow, continued to live there until her death in 1597, when, in accordance with Hill's will, the tenancy was to go to Henry, Abraham Sturley's eldest son, after ten years.[1] Many of the other houses in Wood Street, which were mostly erected on half burgages and lived in by the middling sort, were also damaged or destroyed by the fire and were gradually rebuilt, with tiles replacing the thatch.

At its west end, Wood Street opens out into the wide space of Rother Market. Not surprisingly, since it was the site of the cattle market, husbandmen and yeomen made up a large proportion of the tenants.[2] At its north end stood King's House, now the White Swan, then, as now, kept as an inn. Stretching westward from King's House and consisting of a few small tenements among closes and barns, stood Greenhill Street, referred to in Winter's map as Moor Towns End, but known by the former name in the sixteenth century as it is today. Ely Street too contained dwelling places and barns. As late as the 1570s there were plots of land on which no buildings had been erected. By 1595, tenements had not only been built there but had been destroyed by fire.[3] They were gradually replaced in the early seventeenth century. Tinkers' Lane, running parallel to Ely Street, contained tenements, the rent from which had been earmarked well before the sixteenth century for the benefit of the almsfolk. In 1604 their income from it was 15*s* 10*d*.[4]

Henley Street contained mainly dwelling houses. They were of all sizes and were interspersed by a few barns. There was also a horse mill and a smithy and, of course, the house of John Shakespeare, later the inn called the Maidenhead and now known as Shakespeare's Birthplace. The inhabitants of the street followed a variety of occupations although, during our period, four glovers and three drapers lived there. The lane known as Wynsor, and also as Henley Lane or Hell Lane, lay at its west end and contained four closes and an orchard as well as barns. To own or rent a property in Wynsor seems to have been a sign of status since all the tenants were men of standing in the town. Meer Street, at the other end of Henley Street, had water running through it, as did many of the other streets. However, the Meer Street stream was, perhaps, the largest. People were referred to as living at 'Meer pool side'. The other lanes which made up the borough, Evesham Lane and Mill Lane, contained closes and crofts owned by townsmen, and one large close which belonged to the almspeople.[5]

Although the layout of the centre of the town, with the addition of Union Street and minus Middle Row, remains the same today as in the sixteenth century, the appearance and the atmosphere would have been very different. Many of the streets, only partly paved, had streams running through them, taking rain water, effluent and, no doubt, rubbish down to the river. It was up to the inhabitants of the street to ensure that these watercourses did not incommode pedestrians. In 1608 all the inhabitants of Sheep Street were presented at Quarter Sessions for the decaying of the causeway in their street 'to the hindrance of passengers and the disgrace of the whole burrowe'.[6] At the same time, the inhabitants of Rother Street 'from Mr John Lane's to Mr Gibbs' were presented for not keeping the watercourse scoured, so that it was overflowing. Mr John Gibbs was, at the time, one of the headboroughs of the ward. As well as negotiating the streams, people found other obstructions of an unpleasant nature. Richard Waterman was presented for having a muckhill in Tinkers' Lane without sufficient fence, to the annoyance of 'passengers' and the apparent endangering of children and others. Although one or two people were licensed to keep a muckhill, many more were not and, in the same presentment, there are references to unauthorized muckhills outside the Swan, at the corner of the woodyard towards Bridge-end 'to the great annoyance of travellers, both foot and horsemen', two in Church Street and one at the Bull Ring (at the top end of Sheep Street).

As well as these unsightly, noxious obstructions, attracting stray pigs as well as flies, travellers on foot or horseback had to contend with other difficulties. John Sadler had erected a rail outside his dwelling house in Church Street which was 'a hindrance to passengers', and the Corporation sometimes had to fine a tenant for allowing an outhouse to extend into the common highway. These outhouses were a common feature of the town, several being crammed into the backyards, or backsides as they were usually known. The inventories list couch houses, where barley was spread to dry, malt and mill houses, and kiln houses, where barley was turned into malt. Brewing was carried out in the yeeling house. There were boulting houses for sieving, and grain, garner, hay and fuel houses for storage. There were stables and pig and poultry houses, and sheds containing spinning wheels, harness, ladders and agricultural tools as well as 'trumpery and trash'.

The houses which lined the streets were of all sizes and faced in all directions. Some were joined together in a terrace as in High Street. Some were detached like New Place, the house to which Shakespeare retired, or Hall's Croft, the home of his son-in-law, the physician John Hall. Some were divided between families, as in the case of the house in Henley Street where Shakespeare was born, where, after 1600, the greater part was let and run as the Maidenhead inn while the west end housed Shakespeare's sister, Joan Hart, and her family. What is clear from an inventory of the inn made in 1627 is that the Harts' portion was very small indeed.

A redeeming feature among the sheds, muckhills and ditches was the proliferation of closes, gardens, orchards and, above all, trees.

Hall's Croft, the house in Old Town, Stratford, where William Shakespeare's son-in-law, the physician John Hall, is thought to have lived with his wife, Susannah, whom he married in 1607. Their only daughter, Elizabeth, was probably born here. John Hall died in 1635.

Periodically the Corporation instigated surveys of the trees on their properties with a view to cutting some down in order that the timber might be sold, since wood was an important material for industry as well as for building and fuel. In 1602 eight trees were sold to John Pace for 56s 8d and thirty-two elms to Richard Ingrams for £6.[7] Nevertheless, many trees remained to give pleasure and shade to the town.

What of the people who lived in these streets? What sort of accommodation did they have in their houses and how much did that accommodation cost?

There were four main methods of maintaining a roof over one's head. Freeholders came in two categories: those who inherited a house and those affluent enough to purchase one. Then there were those who rented their accommodation and who might be the direct tenants of the freeholder or sub-tenants of the lessee. Perhaps the most fortunate townsfolk were the freeholders who yearly paid the chief rent of 12d per burgage to the lord of the manor, and who lived in the house erected on that burgage or burgages. George Whateley, woollen draper, paid 12d each year for a burgage in Henley Street on which his house was built. This house contained a hall, two parlours, four chambers and two butteries. The outhouses consisted of a boulting house, two garner houses and a stable, and there was a garden. In his will, made in 1593, he stipulated that his third wife, Joan, should remain there until his son, William, attained the age of twenty-one or married. William, Joan's stepson, was ten years old at the time and, although this might make for friction eleven years later, the chances were that Joan would either remarry or come to an amicable agreement with her stepson. William was assured of a fine house at low cost. The same sort of provision was made by John Sadler senior, who paid the chief rent of 3s 3d for burgages in Church Street where there were three tenements and a garden. Two of these tenements were sub-let but the other tenement and the garden were for his personal use. In his will, made in 1583, he left his younger son, John, 'the house wherein I dwell' with barns, stables, buildings, dovehouse, orchards and garden, after the decease of his wife, Joan. His elder son, Thomas, was left the Bear Inn which his father also owned.[8] Joan Sadler remarried two years later and her second husband was Thomas Dixon alias Waterman, who was the host at the other large inn, the Swan.[9] John Sadler junior was then able to move from the house he occupied in Rother Street and enjoy his patrimony.

There are several extant deeds referring to the sale of houses and, in most cases, the purchaser became responsible for the chief rent as well. In 1582 Christopher Smith alias Court, a yeoman, and his wife, Margery, purchased a tenement in Middle Row, from Thomas Atford of Henley-in-Arden, for £19.[10] The purchaser became responsible for the chief rent of 6d (half a burgage). The house consisted of a hall, two parlours, a kitchen and a buttery, with a loft above. Four years later, Christopher Smith left the house, in his will, to Margery for life and then to his eldest son, John, and his heirs. If John died without heirs the property was to go to the second son, William, and his heirs and, failing that, to the next son, Richard. In 1587 Margery remarried, her second husband being Rafe Lorde, butcher. In 1588 the Lordes leased the property to Richard Lane, gentleman, and Richard Ange, baker, for twenty-one years, stipulating that the rent was to be paid to two of Christopher Smith's daughters, although there is no record of either John's or William's death.[11] In 1609, Margery Lorde, once more a widow, together with her third son, Richard Smith and his wife, sold the Middle Row property to a consortium consisting of four aldermen, for the sum of £30.[12]

Another example of a sale was that of a tenement in Henley Street, sold in 1602 by Elizabeth Quiney, widow, to Thomas Allen, baker, for £60.[13] Thomas was already living in the house and Mistress Quiney had been his landlord. She was the daughter and heir of Thomas Phillips who had left her a considerable amount of property in

Stratford. She married Richard Quiney and jointly they owned property throughout the town. Richard was killed in 1602 when, as bailiff, he tried to stop an affray. Elizabeth became a wealthy and influential widow. In 1611, together with her son, Adrian, she sold yet another messuage, this time in Wood Street, to William Mountford, wheelwright, for £131.[14] William had also been the sitting tenant. We do not know the sizes of these two houses, but we do know that Allen's house was on half a burgage, yet cost twice as much as that of Christopher Smith in 1582, or as another tenement in Bridge Street, for which Thomas Godwin in 1583 paid 40 marks (£26 13s 4d) to his father, Richard Godwin of Tiddington.[15] Although the evidence is slim, it does appear that house prices rose throughout the period.

Owner/occupiers were in the minority. Most of Stratford's inhabitants lived in rented accommodation. Among those who rented directly from the freeholder we find tenants of Elizabeth and Richard Quiney, such as John Ange, baker, who in 1573 rented his tenement in Henley Street from 'the heirs of Thomas Phillips'; or Thomas Smith, tailor, who rented his tenement and outhouses in Sheep Street for twenty-one years at 16s per annum, from Francis and Anne Welshe of 'Cheldesley', Worcestershire, who paid 2s 11d chief rent for various properties in that street.[16] Occasionally the tenant was expected to include the chief rent in his annual payment. This was the case with both Joan Hart, Shakespeare's sister, and Lewis Hiccox, the innkeeper of the Maidenhead. Their landlord was Susannah Hall, Shakespeare's daughter. According to Shakespeare's will, his sister, Joan, had to pay just 12d a year rent for her part of the Henley Street property. Although we do not know the amount of Hiccox's rent, it was clearly much more. However, in 1637, Widow Hart was also paying 12d chief rent and Henry Hiccox, who had taken over the Maidenhead, was paying 1s 10d.[17]

The freeholder and landlord about which most is known was the Corporation itself. The houses which had belonged to the Gild of the

Holy Cross had become the property of the Corporation under the charter of 1553. Many of the indentures recording the leases of these houses have been preserved and provide information as to lessee, his occupation, where the property was situated, how much rent was to be paid and for how long.[18] The lessees were of two kinds: those who did not require the property to live in but intended to sub-let, and those who dwelt in the house which they rented direct from the Corporation.

The former were usually members of the ruling oligarchy who could supplement their income by charging their sub-tenants considerably more than they themselves paid in rent. In only two of these cases do we know the rent charged by the lessee. In 1593, George Whateley, an alderman, left his daughter, Katherine, the lease of a house in High Street where John Fisher lived. This was a house he had held on lease from the Corporation since 1562 at a yearly rent of 26s 8d. It was destroyed by fire in 1595 and Katherine and her husband, Thomas Kirby, agreed to rebuild and were granted a 41-year lease at the old rent. They then leased it to Robert Fisher, John's son, at a rent of 33s 4d. The other example is that of Widow Baylis who paid an annual rent of 6s 8d. The Corporation agreed in 1608 that she should sub-let it to her husband's ex-apprentice, at a yearly rent of 13s 4d.[19]

The clearest indication of the property situation in Stratford can be gained by studying the leases granted by the Corporation to the sitting tenants, particularly in those cases where the tenant's inventory is extant and the rooms in his dwelling house have been enumerated. Nineteen such cases exist and we can see from a study of these in Table 1 that the rents charged had little to do with the amount of accommodation provided. Of course, we do not know the condition of the houses involved, nor the sizes of the rooms; nevertheless it is surprising to learn that, while Rafe Boote, buttonmaker, of Bridge Street, paid 20s rent for a house consisting of a hall, a chamber, a shop and a buttery, Richard Baylis, a fuller, in nearby Middle Row, paid 6s 8d for similar accommodation; and that, while William Smith, mercer, paid 12s rent for a house in Henley Street containing a hall, two parlours, five chambers, a kitchen and a spence, William Homes, weaver, paid only 4s a year less for his two-roomed tenement in Sheep Street.

Over the sixty years the Corporation rents remained much the same. Only if a barn was converted by the tenant, with the Corporation's permission, into one or more tenements, or a house, destroyed by fire, was rebuilt, again by the tenant, on a slightly grander scale, was the rent increased. The total received from borough properties in 1577 was £57 5s 8½d and in 1625 £56 15s 0d. However, there was a hidden increase over the years, for, whenever a new lease was granted, the Corporation was at liberty to charge a fine. It did not always do so, particularly if the house had been destroyed by fire and the tenant agreed to rebuild. Often leases did not run their full term but were surrendered and a new lease, possibly for a longer period, was drawn up. Again there seems little correlation between the length of lease, rent charged and fine imposed. A house in Bridge Street, which remained in the Ange family's occupation for the whole period, was leased in 1575 for twenty-one years at 20s rent for a fine of £10. A new lease was drawn up in 1596 on the same terms. It was surrendered in 1611 for a lease of thirty-one years at the same rent for a fine of £16, and seven years later a fourth lease for sixty-one years was granted for £15. However, on the whole, the most usual progression was for fines and lengths of lease to increase between 1570 and 1630. It is hard to dismiss the suspicion that pressure was brought to bear on existing tenants to surrender their leases in exchange for longer ones (and larger fines) whenever the Corporation felt in need of extra money.

Although the Corporation frowned on 'strangers' being given house room, it did not object to a tenant sharing the house with another Stratford family. Richard Ballamy, locksmith, made a will in 1580 leaving the lease of the house in which he dwelt in Church Street, and for which he paid a yearly rent of 7s 6d, to his wife, Katherine, except that part of the house in which his brother, Thomas, a labourer, lived.[20] This, together with part of the garden and yard, was to remain in Thomas's hands, rent free. He was to repair it at his own charge as long as the lease lasted. Thomas did not carry out his part of the bargain. A Corporation survey made in November 1582 reported that the part of the tenement in the tenure of Katherine Ballamy was sufficiently repaired but Thomas's part was in decay and lacked a chimney in the kitchen.[21] Thomas's share of the house was, apparently, two rooms, and, at the time of his brother's death, he had four children, the youngest being two years old. Richard's share of the house was two rooms as well as a kitchen and shop, but Katherine and Richard had no children, although, as a smith, he may well have had an apprentice. Living conditions must have been very cramped.

Arthur Boyce, tailor, owned his own house but this, too, was shared between members of the family. In his will, Arthur stipulated that his wife, Anne, should have the use of four chambers on the upper floor during her widowhood, paying a rent of 4s to his executor (his son, Francis), and that his son, John, should have that part of the house he then possessed, paying a yearly rent of 13s 4d. At the time, John and Ales (Alice), his wife, had three children under five. According to Arthur's inventory, all his goods were contained in his hall, parlour and one chamber. It does seem as though Francis, as residuary legatee, would have the use of that hall and parlour and perhaps some other rooms, so that there is a possibility that three families lived in what, however, seems to have been a spacious house.

Whether the houses were owner-occupied or rented, spacious or cramped, all were constructed on much the same plan. The hall, which was the general living and eating area, was entered directly from outside. Other rooms, if any, leading off the hall, were referred to as parlours and usually contained bedsteads. Most houses had a kitchen or buttery or both and some had food storage areas such as a spence or a tavern. On the first floor were the bedchambers, one room leading out of another so that there was little privacy. Some houses had a second floor, referred to as a loft or cockloft, and here bacon and grain were stored and, quite often, the presence of bedding in inventories indicated that the servants slept there too.

Table 1 lists all the householders, both tenants and owner-occupiers, within the borough whose inventories show the number of rooms in which they dwelt. Because the information has been presented in as concise a way as possible, several aspects of it need to be clarified.

The rents shown are those paid annually to the Corporation with two exceptions. Matthew Baylis was apprentice to his kinsman, Richard Baylis. In 1608 Matthew, now a married man with two daughters, became the under-tenant of Richard's widow and is the only person on the list for whom information about his accommodation was found in the inventory of another's goods. Arthur Newell, although referred to as yeoman, was under-tenant of the Angel Inn in Back Bridge Street, for which Arthur Cawdry, woollen draper, paid a rent of 33s 4d to the Corporation. This accounts for the large number of beds and the small number in Newell's immediate household.

Parlours and solars, in both of which beds were usually found, have been included under the heading 'chambers'. The numbers in brackets show the number of bedsteads in the inventory. The types of bed and sleeping arrangements will be discussed in Chapter Three. Where a plus sign appears after the number of chambers, the heading in the inventory is 'in the other chambers'. 'Kitchens' include butteries and spences. Such rooms as cocklofts, cellars, malt chambers, corn chambers and taverns come under the heading 'others', while outhouses include stables and barns.

It is the calculation of the sizes of households which requires most clarification. The exact number can only be a matter of speculation, except in those cases listed in a presentment of the names of all maltsters and victuallers made in 1595.[22] In that document household size is specifically stated. There are nine cases in which this is so, but

Table 1. Accommodation in dwelling places within the borough, 1570–1630.

Householder	Rent	Hall	Chambers	Kitchens	Others	O/h	H/h
William Bainton*	20s 0d	1	3 (4)	2	–	–	4
Richard Baker, draper	–	1	3 (5)	1	–	2	7
Richard Baylis, fuller	6s 8d	1	2 (3)	–	shop	–	3
Matthew Baylis, fuller	13s 4d	1	2	–	shop	–	4
Richard Ballamy, smith	7s 6d	1	2 (4)	1	shop	–	8
Thomas Ballamy, labourer							
Joan Biddle, widow	8s 0d	1	4 (5)	2	–	1	7
Rafe Boote, buttonmaker	20s 0d	1	1 (6)	1	shop	–	6
Arthur Boyce, tailor	Own	1	5 (3+)	–	–	–	7
Richard Boyce, tailor	14s 0d	1	6 (6)	2	2	–	6
Edward Bromley, carrier	–	1	2 (2+)	–	–	–	4
John Brown, draper	Own	1	3 (6)	2	–	5	7
John Coxe, shepherd	6s 8d	1	2 (1)	1	–	–	3
Richard Dawkes, plumber	–	1	3 (4)	1	–	–	5
Henry Field, tanner	10s 0d	1	4 (5)	1	–	1	9
John Gibbs, gent	16s 0d	1	4+ (7)	2	–	1	7
Wm. Greenway, carrier	13s 4d	1	4 (5)	–	shop	1	7
Ann Hiccox, widow	20s 0d	1	6 (5)	2	shop	3+	10
Lewis Hiccox, innkeeper	–	1	7 (13)	1	3	1	6+
Thomas Hiccox, yeoman	6s 8d	1	3 (4)	1	1	3	4
William Homes, weaver	8s 0d	1	1 (0)	–	–	–	4
Richard Hornby, smith	Own	1	1 (2)	2	–	–	7
Robert Hynd, chapman	16s 0d	1	2 (3)	–	shop	–	4
Robert Ingram, fisherman	–	1	1 (3)	1	–	2	10
Robert Johnson, innkeeper	6s 8d	1	8 (19)	–	3	4	9+
Mary Mills, widow	20s 0d	1	3 (2)	2	–	1	3
Arthur Newell, yeoman	33s 4d	1	5 (8)	2	–	–	3+
John Page, ironmonger	–	1	3 (1)	–	–	–	unwed
Humfrey Plymley, draper	16s 0d	1	2 (1)	2	–	–	3
William Rogers, sergeant	10s 0d	1	7 (6)	2	–	3	6

(continued overleaf)

Householder	Rent	Hall	Chambers		Kitchens	Others	O/h	H/h
Michael Shacleton, clothworker	–	1	2	(3)	–	–	–	4
Ralph Shawe, wooldriver	Own	1	2	(5)	–	1	1	5
Christopher Smith, yeoman	Own	1	2	(20)	2	1	–	7
Daniel Smith, yeoman	Own	1	3	(4)	2	–	4	4
William Smith, mercer	12s 0d	1	7	(5)	2	–	–	12
William Smith jr., mercer	Own	1	3	(4)	1	–	–	6+
William Trowte, butcher	29s 4d	1	5	(4)	1	shop	–	4
Edward Wakeland, yeoman	–	1	2	(2)	1	1	–	4
George Whateley, draper	Own	1	6	(6)	2	–	4	5+
Richard Whiting, yeoman	Own	1	5	(8)	1	2	1	5+
Thomas Wotton, weaver	–	1	3	(5)	–	shop	–	4

Key: O/h = Outhouses

H/h = Number in household

* The occupation of William Bainton is not known

even here it is likely that this is not the maximum number of persons who had lived in the house at any one time. For instance, Richard Boyce had certainly lived in his house in High Street since his marriage in 1560. He had brought up nine children and, in 1576, probably five sons and a daughter were living at home. In his will he mentions Cyrell Williams, his serving maid, to whom he left a quarter of malt, and, as a tailor, he very probably had an apprentice. This would mean that thirteen people could have been living in the house in the 1570s although, by 1595, most of his children would have been out to service and the six chambers in his house would no longer echo to the noise and bustle of twenty years earlier.

On the other hand, John Gibbs, who had also lived in his house in Rother Street since his first marriage in 1567, had no children, so that the five extra persons in his household in 1595 must have been

Mason's Court, Rother Street, one of the oldest surviving domestic buildings in Stratford. In the sixteenth century it was occupied by Master John Gibbs from the time of his first marriage in 1567 until his death in 1625.

servants, although a note at the end of his will, made in 1622, might give an indication of another explanation for at least one other person in the household. It states that Gibbs's brother-in-law, John Lane, still owed him £15 for 'tabling his daughter Katharine' for five years and more at £5 a year. It seems unlikely that the debt was outstanding for twenty-seven years and that Katharine had been living with the Gibbs in 1595, but it could be that she was not the only young girl to have been 'tabled' in the Gibbs household. The practice of parents arranging for children or young adults to live with another family, quite usual among the aristocracy, is not mentioned in any other Stratford document, although reasons for it are not difficult to imagine. A second marriage might cause friction between a step-parent and any older children; one child less in the house might relieve overcrowding; or, in some cases, hope for the social advancement of the child might be the guiding factor. Perhaps the Gibbs, having no children of their own, had welcomed their niece as an attractive addition to their household.

In the cases where the size of the household is not specified in the 1595 document, the circumstances of the householder have been carefully studied and, if it is known that the family had lived in the house for many years, the household size has been calculated as the parents plus the number of children under fourteen at any one time, plus an apprentice if the householder was a craftsman, and a maidservant if the inventory mentions a 'maid's chamber'. The tendency has been to err on the conservative side, disregarding the possible presence of elderly relatives, extra apprentices or serving men. To give just one example, George Whateley, woollen draper, who left £105 worth of goods and owned his own substantial house, had two children under fourteen when he died in 1595.[23] The other members of the household were their stepmother, Joan, and, since there was a maid's chamber in the inventory, a servant. But that chamber contained two bedsteads although only one mattress, and another chamber contained bedding, so that more than one servant is a distinct possibility, particularly as George Whateley was wealthy by Stratford standards. In Table 1 his household has been calculated at 5+.

Table 2 lists the accommodation known to have been enjoyed by those living outside the borough. Here the information is not so plentiful or detailed. We do not know the rents charged or whether the householder owned his house. Household size has had to be calculated on numbers of children under fourteen at any one time and the inclusion of a servant's chamber in the inventory or a servant mentioned in a will. Richard Barbur, yeoman, of Drayton, left 12*d* to 'each household servant', 5 marks to John Carpenter 'a little boy in my

Table 2. Accommodation in dwelling places outside the borough, 1570–1630.

Householder	Hall	Chambers	Kitchens	Others	O/h	H/h
Richard Barbur, yeoman, Drayton	1	2(5)	1	–	1	8
Richard Barbur, husbandman, Drayton	1	2(4)	1	–	1	8
William Baule, labourer, Bishopton	1	1(0)	–	–	–	10
Roger Burman, husbandman, Shottery	1	1(3)	1	–	–	6
Nicholas Checket,* Bridgetown	1	2(3)	1	–	–	?
John Dibdale, husbandman, Shottery	1	1(4)	1	–	–	8
Bartholomew Hathaway, yeoman, Shottery	1	4(3)	1	–	++	8
Thomas Hiccox, husbandman, Welcombe	1	+(3)	–	–	2	7+
Robert Johnson, yeoman, Old Stratford	1	4(2)	–	–	1	3
John Marshall, curate, Bishopton	1	3(5)	1	–	2	6
Robert Munmore, husbandman, Shottery	1	3(3)	1	–	3	6+
Elizabeth Pace, widow, Shottery	1	1(2)	1	–	–	?
Richard Pace, husbandman, Shottery	1	1(3)	1	–	–	?
John Richardson, yeoman, Shottery	1	2(3)	1	–	–	10
Elizabeth Smart, widow, Bishopton	1	2(2)	–	–	1	?
William Such,* Shottery	1	1(3)	1	–	–	8
William Taylor, labourer, Old Stratford	1	1(2)	–	–	–	4
William Whittorne, carpenter, Old Stratford	1	1(1)	–	–	–	2

Key: O/h = Outhouses
H/h = Number in household

household', and 20s to Sycelley Smythe, 'my servant'. He had one son, aged seventeen, who was his heir, and probably helped his father with the considerable amount of farm stock. The number in his household would seem to be at least eight, and possibly more, at the time of his death. Where no indication of household size is given, no attempt has been made to calculate one. The overall picture is of fairly small dwelling places, containing hall and kitchen and never more than four chambers, and no other rooms. Doubtless there were other outhouses than those listed, but only those mentioned in the inventories have been included in the table.

In order to retain a roof over one's head and not become one of the homeless poor, an income was necessary. Like the living accommodation in Stratford, there was a wide variation in the occupations of the townsfolk and the rewards gained thereby, and these will be the subjects of the next chapter.

CHAPTER TWO

OCCUPATIONS AND FINANCES

The said Towne is now fallen much into decay for want of such trade as heretofore they have had by clothinge and makinge of yarne ymploying And maynteyninge a number of poor people by the same, which now live in great penury and myserie by reason they are not set a work as before.[1]

So reads a petition of the Corporation of Stratford-upon-Avon to Lord Treasurer Burghley in 1590. We must allow for the possibility that, as it was a petition, some exaggeration may have been employed, but it was true that the popular new draperies such as cambric and lawn, which were being manufactured in East Anglia by refugees from the Low Countries, were gradually ousting the heavier woollens which were still being produced and sold by most of the weavers and drapers of Stratford.

The 800 persons who are being put under the microscope in this study consist of 631 men and 169 women. Of these, we know the primary occupations of 461 (including twenty-one women). Between them they cover sixty-nine different occupations. Apart from workers on the land, the largest group is that of the tailors, closely followed by the glovers, weavers and shoemakers. These were all craftsmen or craftsmen/traders. Among those who just traded, the largest groups are the drapers and the mercers, general merchants dealing mainly in cloth.

The outlying hamlets which made up the parish of Stratford stood among the fields which surrounded the town. It is not surprising, then, that the majority of persons living in these hamlets worked on the land. Although 113 of our total lived outside the borough, the occupations or standings of only fifty-two have been specifically stated in documents and forty-three of those were in agriculture. Of these, sixteen were yeomen, thirteen husbandmen, four labourers and ten were gentlemen with considerable holdings in agricultural land. When we look at the inventories, however, we find that, even among those whose occupations we do not know, the greater part of their wealth was in farm stock and cereals. For instance, John Edwards of Drayton, whose livestock, cereals and farming implements accounted for 85 per cent of his goods, must be assumed to have been a farmer.

What may seem surprising is the fact that a large number of dwellers in the town also counted working the land as their main

Table 3. Primary occupations, 1570–1630.*

Craftsmen and craftsmen/traders

24 tailors	2 tugerers
23 glovers	2 spinsters
23 butchers	2 clothworkers
20 weavers	2 woolwinders
16 shoemakers	2 tilers
15 bakers	2 dyers
15 carpenters	1 painter
12 smiths	1 cutler
7 skinners	1 buttonmaker
7 fullers	1 plumber
6 tanners	1 fletcher
6 saddlers	1 collarmaker
5 wheelwrights	1 cardmaker
5 haberdashers	1 ploughwright
4 millers	1 thatcher
3 coopers	1 fisherman
2 masons	1 tinker
2 farriers	

Traders
18 drapers
14 mercers
5 ironmongers
3 chandlers
2 corndealers
2 wooldrivers
2 vintners
1 pedlar
1 fishmonger

Workers on the land
60 yeomen
25 husbandmen
14 labourers
6 shepherds

Services
18 victuallers
13 clerics
12 lawyers

9 innkeepers
9 servants
6 schoolmasters
4 maltsters
4 sergeants-at-mace
2 scriveners
2 carriers
1 beadle
1 gardener
1 keeper of clocks
1 physician
1 musician
1 bailiff
1 barber
1 surgeon
1 apothecary
1 playwright
1 gravemaker

28 gentlemen

---

*   Several occupations, although basically the same, had more than one name. To make for clarity, such occupations have been grouped under one title. These are: glovers (and whittawers), shoemakers (and corvisers), carpenters (and joiners) skinners (and furriers), fullers (walkers and shearmen), haberdashers (and hatters) and smiths (and locksmiths). Of the two 'clothworkers', one was a weaver of hair cloth which was used to hold the barley over the furnace in malt-making. The other is referred to merely as a 'clothworker'. The term 'tugerer' is obscure but is believed to mean one who prepares the roof for the thatcher. Wooldrivers, known as woolbroggers in some other parts of the country, were the middlemen buying the raw wool and selling it to be made into cloth.

occupation. These are men who, although living within the borough and possibly following some other occupation as well, such as corndealing, butchering or milling, thought of themselves, or were regarded by their contemporaries, as primarily gaining their livelihood from agriculture, being referred to as either husbandmen or yeomen and either working their holdings in the surrounding fields themselves, or employing, or being employed by, others to do so. The title of yeoman was normally given to the more successful of these farmers and a study of their inventories largely supports this definition.

Table 3 (pages 22–3) sets out a comprehensive list of the sixty-nine primary occupations and the numbers employed in each one.[2] They fall into four categories – craftsmen and craftsmen/traders, traders, workers on the land, and what could loosely be called the service industries, which last include innkeepers, victuallers, lawyers, doctors, clerics, etc. The word 'primary' has been used advisedly, for many people had a secondary occupation and some even a third. Edward Hunte, designated yeoman, was also a corndealer, and William Gilbard alias Higgs, who was in succession usher, curate and minister, was also keeper of the town clocks in order to supplement his usher's salary of £5 a year. But by far the most usual secondary occupation was victualling – brewing and selling ale. No fewer than fifty-five persons were referred to as victuallers while following another occupation as well.

When, in the 1590s, a series of disastrous harvests created a shortage of cereals, the government instructed local JPs to find out the amount of corn being grown and stored, to restrict brewing and malting and unnecessary victualling, and to ensure that markets were supplied with corn at a price which the poorer sort could afford. In Stratford this resulted in the document, already referred to in Chapter One, entitled: 'A trewe presentment of the names of all the mallsters, buyers & sellers of grayne, Brewers, Bakers & victuallers within this Borough & howses or barnes or else wheare as farre as wee have eyther seene or otherwise

A shoemaker was frequently also a cobbler and both made and mended shoes.

can learn as followeth.' While the first half of this very informative document lists the malt-makers and will be referred to later in this chapter, the second half lists the victuallers of the borough, numbering at that time thirty-seven. Here we read such entries as: 'Edward Aynge usethe his shumakers occupacon. His wieff utterethe by bruyng weekely vi strikes of mallt and are in howshold vii persons', or: 'Foulk Jhonson usethe the art of surgerye. His wieffe utterethe weekely iii strikes of mallte. In howshold iiii persons.' It is clear that, although the men are referred to as the victuallers, it is the wives who brewed and sold (uttered) the ale. Twenty-nine entries specifically mention the wives as the brewers and six widows are described as victuallers in their own right.

Victualling was only one of the ways in which women contributed to the economy of the town. Many would have tended the livestock, in particular the pigs, chickens and ducks which many households kept in their 'backsides'. On a much grander scale, some widows, both within and without the town, continued to carry on their husbands' agricultural activities although, no doubt, employing others to do the heavy work. Katherine Salisbury, widow of a yeoman, who lived within the borough, left cereals and livestock amounting to 75 per cent of her total goods of £95. Elizabeth Such, a widow of Bishopton, left 'a hachet a bill 2 shepickes a doungforke and a nawger' (12*d*), '2 wheles and a paier of hewing blades' (6*d*), '2 harrowes and a mattoke' (2*s*), 'in the barne whete and barley' (£4), 'feches and hey' (6*s* 8*d*), 'a kowe and a heyfer' (40*s*), '2 geese & a gander xii hennes & a cocke' (3*s* 4*d*) and '2 store pidgs' (3*s* 4*d*), and these were out of a total of under £18.

Of the twenty-one women whose occupation is specifically stated, there were nine who were single. Of these, six were servants, two of whom married later, and two were referred to as spinsters, although it is not clear whether this means that they did spinning for a living, or were just unmarried, for most women spun yarn for household use and

Many inventories listed one or more spinning wheels. Both wool and flax were spun into yarn by the women of the house.

almost every inventory lists at least one spinning wheel. However, when she made her will in 1624, Avis Clark referred to herself as spinster and, from her bequests, was clearly unmarried. Yet, although those who compiled her inventory did not mention any occupation for her, the items listed show that she was, in fact, a pedlar, and, apart from her wearing apparel and an old pair of sheets and a blanket, her total worldly goods, amounting to £3, consisted of her pedlar's wares. These include such items as 'six hancarchonds . . . ii^s', 'sixe peare of gartares . . . iii^s' and 'forty to yardes of bonlase . . . iiii^s'. In her will she is described as 'of Stratford upon Avon', although in the burial register she is a 'stranger' (someone from outside the area). She seems to have made Stratford her base since all her bequests were to Stratfordians.

Of the twelve widows whose occupations we know, eight were victuallers and one a maltster. The remaining three carried on their late husbands' businesses. Richard Ballamy, locksmith, stated in his will 'what debtes be due unto me from others & who they be that owe it my wife Doth knowe by the skores witch she hath of theirs'. After his death Katharine Ballamy employed a smith but continued to run the business. Alice Ange ran her late husband's bakery business in conjuction with their son, Francis, and was referred to as 'Widow Ange, baker'.[3] Isabel Wotton followed her husband's occupation as weaver. In his will, Thomas Wotton left 20*s* to the use and maintenance of the box belonging to his occupation (the funds of his trade guild) 'in consideration that they shall be guides unto my wife during her widowhood'.[4] Although these three widows are the only ones referred to as continuing their husbands' occupations, this was not an uncommon practice. When Richard Baylis, fuller and shearman, left his apprentice and kinsman, Matthew Baylis, a pair of shears for his occupation, he stipulated that his own wife, Isabel, should first choose two of the best pairs for herself; and the rules of some of the trading companies allowed for the widow's occupation. For instance, the rules of the local Shoemakers' and Saddlers' Company set down that, if his master died, an apprentice might serve out his years with his master's widow, and a widow of a company member might carry on his craft. A second marriage to a non-member of the guild required permission if they wished to continue the trade.[5]

Many families had one or more maidservants who carried out domestic duties, learned to spin and knit, and helped to tend any livestock. Girls were indentured at the age of fourteen (earlier if they were orphaned) and remained with their mistress's family for seven years or longer.

A stage in the craft of clothmaking: a shearman at work.

The inventory of Richard Baylis, fuller and shearman, who died in 1606 aged forty-eight. Although here the name is spelt 'Balys', on other documents it is spelt 'Balis', 'Bailies' and 'Baylis'. Variations in spelling, particularly of surnames, constantly occur.

The single women who were servants had probably been indentured when they were fourteen. This was common practice and, if they did not marry when their seven years' service ended, they often stayed on with the family. Many were left small legacies in their masters' or mistresses' wills. Daniel Baker, the influential puritan woollen draper, outlived his children and, when he made his will in 1637, he left 20*s* to Ellinor Roberts, late servant to his daughter-in-law, Elizabeth Baker, deceased, 'in regard to her love to my grandchildren'.

Orphans were indentured as servants or put to learn a trade well before they were fourteen. In 1604, Thomas Ravens, corviser, and his wife, Joan, undertook, for the sum of 40*s* paid to them by the Churchwardens and Overseers of the Poor, to take in the orphan daughter of John Atwood, tailor, also Joan, aged nine years. They promised to teach her knitting, weaving of bone lace 'and other honeste trades of life as they now use'.[6] Mary, Joan's elder sister, was indentured at eleven years old, to Robert Butler, whittawer, and Alice his wife, for ten years, to serve as 'spinster or maid servant'.[7] Among the orphan boys, ten-year-old Thomas Saull was covenanted servant for nine years to John Johnsons, glover. Another, Thomas Fynche, covenanted at thirteen years of age to Richard Jones, tailor, became his master's heir and eventually married the daughter of the house in true folk-tale tradition.[8]

Under normal circumstances boys as well as girls left home at fourteen to be apprenticed or become covenanted servants with another family. Usually they remained in or near Stratford, although one or two left the area. Isabel Bardall wrote to her 'cozen' Richard Quiney, then in London on Corporation business, asking him to seek out a place for her son with some handycraft man. Apparently the boy had been with her cousin Parker who had replaced him with another and Isabel complained, 'I can gett noe place for hym in the contrey.'[9] Those who remained in the town entered into an agreement with their masters to serve well and faithfully for seven years:

Harlottes, dice, cardes or unhonest company or places suspected or games forbidden he shall not frequente. Matrymony with any woman within the seyd terme he shall not contracte, nether comyt any carnall facte [sic] with any mayde servant of his seyd master.[10]

In return the master undertook to teach him his trade, providing him with meat, drink, linen, woollen, bedding, hose, shoes, etc. Once he had served his apprenticeship and, perhaps, spent some time as journeyman, he could pay his fine and be accepted into the relevant trade company with the freedom to set up on his own. If he had served his apprenticeship in the borough, the fee for entry into his company was only 3s 4d, but 'foreigners' had to pay £4 on entry and then only if the master of the company gave permission. If someone born in the town had served his apprenticeship elsewhere then the fee was £1. Half of all these fines went into the Corporation's coffers.

A tailor cuts out a garment while his apprentices sew.

Although the woollen trade in Stratford was on the decline, there was another trade which was flourishing. In the first half of the document which lists maltsters and victuallers, a typical entry reads: 'July Shawe usethe the trades of buyinge and selling of woll and yorne And maltinge and hathe in house xviii quarters and halfe of mallte and x quarters of barley whereof xx stryke of the mallte is Mr Watkyns Mr Grevylls mans and v quarters of one Gylbardes of Roddytche and the rest his own. There are in howshold iii persons.' In a different hand: 'To bringe to the markete iiii stryke a weeke to Stretforde and xii to Brymingham.' Four columns at the side list the amount of malt, barley, wheat and peas in the householder's possession.

There are sixty-seven names which include many of the most important men of the borough, such as Richard Quiney, alderman and soon to be bailiff, who 'usethe the trades of buying and sellinge corn for great sommes', and Richard Woodward, gentleman, owner of lands in Quinton, Butlers Marston and Shottery as well as in the town. The list is headed by Thomas Rogers, 'now baieliefe'.

Clearly many of these maltsters were not poor men eking out a living by making malt for others, but affluent members of Stratford society who found malt-making a paying proposition. Between them they produced more than 1,000 quarters of malt and had in store 525 quarters of barley. They were detailed to send twenty-four quarters of malt a week to Birmingham market and thirteen quarters of malt and five quarters of barley weekly to Stratford market.

In their petition of 1590, quoted at the beginning of this chapter, the bailiff and burgesses may have given the impression that 'clothinge and makinge of yarne' had been the main occupation of Stratford townsfolk, but by 1598 they had changed their tune. In a further petition, this time for toleration with regard to a royal proclamation of 1597 that no malt be brewed between Lady Day and Michaelmas, it was insisted that Stratford had no other especial trade than malting and houses were fitted to no other purposes.[11] So it seems that Richard Quiney was nearer the mark when he wrote that the town 'is auncient in this trading of malteing and have ever served to Birmingham, from whence Walles, Sallop Stafford, Chess and Lanke also are served'.[12]

Certainly it is rare to find a Stratford inventory which does not list malt-making equipment and, when the debts listed in inventories and wills, specifically referring to malt, are studied, together with the 1595 document, we find that several customers came from as far away as Birmingham in the north and Banbury and Hampton, near Evesham, in the south-east and south-west respectively. One or two came from

Harvard House, High Street. The house was built by Master Thomas Rogers, alderman and twice Bailiff, who 'besides his butchers trade which until now of late hee allwaies used . . . ys a buyer and seller of corne for great sommes & withall usethe grazing and buyinge and selling of cattell'. Katharine, one of his eleven daughters, married into the Harvard family and her son founded Harvard University. Thomas's initials, together with those of his second wife, Alice, are carved into the frontage of the house.

even farther afield. Daventry and Little Wenlock are mentioned. For Stratford townsfolk, from the bailiff who 'besydes his butchers trade which untill now of late hee allwaies used hee ys a buyer and seller of corne for great sommes & withall usethe grazinge and buyinge and selling of cattell', with his thirty-five quarters, to the widow Shacleton, who 'bruethe weekelye iii strike of mallte which is her only mayntenance havinge in household iii persons', malt-making was an important, perhaps the most important, occupation. Yet in the documents which form the basis for this study only four persons are specifically called maltsters.

Among those listed as maltsters in the document only one is termed 'gentleman', although several others are entitled 'master' and given no other occupation. One of these is Mr Richard Woodward who 'hathe in his howse x quarters of mallte and v quarters of Barleye And in his barne as wee iudge unthreshte Barley xxxii quarters and of Rye v quarters and are in howshold xxv persons'. Since he also owned property outside the borough his name appears in another similar document under Shottery.[13] This time he is 'Richard Woodward, gentleman'. This exemplifies the difficulty in determining those entitled to style themselves 'gentlemen'. The prefix 'Mr' was given to all aldermen of the borough, but it did not necessarily follow that they were indeed 'gentlemen', although several were by the end of their careers. In the parish registers a man may be called 'Mr' in one place and have 'generosi' (literally, of noble blood, or well-born) in another. According to Peter Laslett, 'the primary characteristic of a gentleman was that he never worked with his hands on necessary, as opposed to leisurely, activities.'[14] Several Stratford worthies clearly did work with their hands. Such a one was Francis Ange, son of Richard Ange, baker. Francis also became a baker and, having served his term as constable, became a capital burgess and, in 1621, an alderman. In 1622 his son Richard was born and the entry in the baptism register reads 'Richard son of Mr Francis Ange'. In 1623, however, the name of his next child was entered in the register as 'Maria filia Francis Ange generosi', although, when his five subsequent children's baptisms were recorded, he was once again 'Mr'. However, his burial entry in 1656 reads: 'Francis Ainge gent'.

In this study such 'new' gentlemen have been listed under their occupations, so that 'Mr William Shakespeare, gentleman' is the playwright in Table 3, and 'Mr Abraham Sturley, gentleman' is one of the corndealers. The twenty-eight who are listed as 'gentlemen' are, as far as can be ascertained, 'gentlemen born', as the young shepherd in *The Winter's Tale* would have it. These include members of the Combe family of Old Stratford and the Lanes, Nashes and Reynolds in the town. They also include Samuel Tyler, whose grandfather, Richard, was a yeoman and whose father, also Richard, was a lawyer. This Mr Richard Tyler was town clerk of Stratford and had been educated at one of the Inns of Court. Legal training was often the alternative to a university education and several Stratford gentlemen had such training, but only if they served in the capacity of lawyers in the town are they included among the twelve lawyers in Table 3. Seventeen men who are termed 'gentleman' at some stage in their lives have been listed under their other occupations, thus bringing the total of gentlemen in this study to forty-five.

The 'gentlemen born' may not have worked with their hands, but several had considerable holdings in the surrounding countryside and, presumably, provided employment for husbandmen, labourers and shepherds. An early inventory shows that Clement Swallow, gentleman, of Shottery, was worth £97 when he died in 1571, and his farm stock and cereals about a quarter of this. The last item in his inventory reads 'Certayne lawe bookes and other bookes wth other tryfles of small value . . . vi[s]', so it seems likely that the young Clement Swallow had attended one of the Inns of Court.

Clement also owned two geldings with saddles and bridles and 'bootes spurres swyrde daggers wth other necessaries for Rydynge'. This is a reminder, should one be needed, of the importance of horses for both travel and agriculture, and horse trading was another activity which benefited Stratford. The charter of 1553 allowed the town to hold two annual fairs, one in May and the other in September. Traders came from as far as a hundred miles away, and for two or three days Stratford was full to capacity. As the town was at the centre of the area stretching from Berkshire to Leicestershire, one of the regions famous for horse fairs, horse trading was an important activity at fair time. Even if the horses were brought from outside the area and sold to, or exchanged with, a 'stranger', the Corporation still collected a toll of 4*d* on each sale and 2*d* on an exchange. Three toll books of horses sold or exchanged during the seventeenth century are still extant. The earliest one, dated 1602, records only ten sales and two exchanges.[15] In it we can read such items as: 'Jo[hn] bleksonne of Ast[o]n sub edge in co. glos. hath sold to Jo[hn] Whit of Morton Morrell in co. War. a whit mare w[th] a sucking bay colt w[th] a blese in the forehead the mare whole eared p[rice] £3.3.4. tole 4*d*.' Most buyers and sellers came from within Warwickshire or from just over the borders in Gloucestershire or Oxfordshire. No one from Stratford itself was involved. The highest sum paid for a horse was £5 4*s* 0*d* and the lowest 3*s* 4*d*. The entire affair seems to have been very low key.

But when we look at the other two toll books, both dated 1646, a very different picture emerges.[16] In all, 450 transactions were made, mostly sales. The prices paid ranged from 14*s* 6*d* for a horse, to £26 for two mares in foal. Both buyers and sellers came from much farther afield – a trader from North Kilworth in Leicestershire, fifty miles from Stratford, made several purchases as well as sales. Others came from Clipston in Northamptonshire and Draycot in Oxfordshire, both fifty miles away. This time several Stratford townsfolk were involved. Daniel Beard of Stratford-upon-Avon, costermonger, sold to Thomas Taylor of 'Ebberton' (Ebrington), Gloucestershire, a bay mare, bald face, four white feet and wall eyes, for £2 16s 0d. The voucher was Richard Edwards of Stratford, baker. The Corporation made over £7 in tolls.

Although 1602 may have been a particularly poor year for the horse trade, and 1646, with the Civil War in progress, a bumper one, the differences between the toll books could be explained by a gradual building up of the trade during the first half of the seventeenth century. As well as bringing toll money into the town's coffers, it would have been of benefit to Stratford in other ways, since it is likely that the traders, having come to the town, would have stayed to spend their money on other goods for sale at the fairs.

Naturally, not all purchasing of horses took place at the fairs. In his will dated 14 November 1578, Roger Sadler, baker, listed the debts due to him.[17] One was from Mr John Combe, the elder, who owed £3 for a horse, and another from Mr Walter Roche for £4 'which I must pay over to brother Skidmore [his brother-in-law of London] for a mare'. Being the owner of one or more horses, although they had to be fed and cared for, could help to supplement one's income. John Lupton, a skinner, was paid 4s by the chamberlain for hiring out his horse for four days.[18]

Such an additional source of income was imperative, particularly for those who worked for a wage. Although, as we shall see later, the prices for food and clothing rose considerably between 1570 and 1630, the wages of craftsmen did not keep pace. The following are a few examples, gleaned from the chamberlains' accounts, for work carried out for the Corporation.[19] In 1570 Basil Burdett, a mason, was paid 2s 2d for two days' work 'laying up stones on the bridge'. Thirty years later another mason, Robert Hall, was paid 14s for two weeks' work 'paving around the High Cross'. In 1585 George Rose, a carpenter, did two days' work for 18d and in 1598 he and his man worked for fourteen days at 21d a day – his man probably earning 9d and George 12d a day. By 1623 'one Francis' a carpenter did five days' work for 5s. Thatchers were working for 1s a day in 1605 and for the same wage in

1623, although this might reflect the fact that, since the fires of the 1590s, thatching had fallen out of favour and the Corporation was insisting on roofs being tiled. Tilers were one set of craftsmen whose wages did rise, although only slightly. In 1580 two tilers worked for four days for 6s 8d (10d a day), but by 1627 another tiler could command 4s 8d for four days' work. It is clear though that, throughout the period, most craftsmen's wages averaged 1s a day. It is unlikely that there would be a constant supply of work throughout the year and, in any case, most crafts would be affected by the weather, so that a yearly wage of between £12 and £15 could be expected.

Unskilled men, naturally, fared worse. In 1580 'the man who served the tilers' worked for 7d a day, and, in 1627, fifty-seven men were employed to work on the stone bridge and were paid sums ranging from 1d to 10d a day.[20] Women, too, were employed to do heavy unskilled work. In 1612, twenty women picked up stones for 5d a day each and, a year earlier, Elizabeth Smith was paid 3d for clearing away the stones and clay from two upper chambers after the masons and tilers had done their work. It has ever been women's lot to clear up after the men!

As their wages did not keep pace with inflation, it is not surprising that, as can be seen in Table 4 (page 40), of the fifty-two craftsmen and craftsmen/traders whose inventories have been studied, forty-six left less than £50 worth of goods and thirty-five less than £25. Inventories are not a comprehensive statement of a man's financial standing since houses and lands which he owned were not included and thus some testators appear less wealthy than was really the case. Leases held are sometimes valued and sometimes not, and, occasionally, such obvious items as wearing apparel are omitted. They do, however, give a reasonable indication of a man's disposable wealth or lack of it.

The six testators who left goods totalling more than £50 who appear in the 'craftsmen' column were, in fact, all craftsmen/traders. William

Table 4. The relationship between occupation and wealth as calculated in 162 inventories 1570–1630.

Amount (£)	Craftsmen and craftsmen/ traders	Workers on the land	Traders	Widows	Unknown	Others
0–1	0	0	0	1	1	0
2–5	7	6	1	3	2	3
6–10	8	2	0	2	2	0
11–15	7	2	1	2	1	0
16–20	8	0	2	4	0	0
21–25	5	2	0	0	1	1
26–30	2	0	0	1	1	1
31–35	0	3	2	3	1	2
36–40	3	3	0	1	0	0
41–45	2	3	0	0	0	0
46–50	4	3	0	0	1	0
51–55	1	2	0	1	0	1
56–60	1	1	0	1	1	0
61–65	0	1	1	1	0	0
66–70	1	0	0	0	1	0
71–75	0	2	0	0	1	1
76–80	1	0	0	1	1	1
81–85	0	5	0	0	0	0
86–90	0	1	1	0	0	0
91–95	1	0	0	0	0	1
96–100	0	2	0	0	0	1
100+	1	6	3	3	1	4

Hobday, glover, left £66 which included £20 worth of various types of leather. Thomas Kirby, butcher, left goods valued at £91 of which 18 per cent was for farm stock, cereals and bees, and over £4 was owed to him. William Smarte, baker, also owned a considerable amount of cereals and livestock which made up 25 per cent of his £76. Thomas Roberts, shoemaker, whose inventory totalled £106, was owed £27 16s 0d by his customers, some of whom came from other counties. The remaining two were a father and son, both tailors, who may well have worked for a wage occasionally. Certainly Richard Boyce was paid 5s for making up two gowns for the sergeants at mace. His £56 worth of goods included over £5 for farm stock and a further £5 worth of malt. His father, Arthur Boyce, left £52, of which £20 was for malt and malt-making equipment and £16 11s 3d were debts owed him for malt and barley.

Among the craftsmen whose wealth was calculated below £50, those in the higher bracket – £35 and over – also used either husbandry or malting as a second occupation. Humfrey Allen, shoemaker, who left goods worth £36, owned farm stock and cereals which made up 63 per cent of his total, while malt and the equipment for making it was worth £34 out of the £47 left by John Page, a smith. Those whose goods totalled less than £10 had no such assets and normally the only items they owned which were not household goods and apparel were tools. Richard Ballamy, locksmith, had £2 worth of tools to set against his £4 worth of goods, and the weaver George Grannams's looms accounted for £1 out of his £6. It seems, then, that the stock-in-trade and the prices customers paid for the finished articles, gave the craftsmen/traders the edge over craftsmen, but that, without a secondary occupation such as malting or husbandry, there was little chance of a craftsman providing his family with more than the bare essentials.

In Table 4, as in Table 3, labourers have been included with those who worked on the land, although, as we have seen, they worked at other tasks, such as assisting craftsmen or working on the stone bridge.

However, it seems likely that agricultural work took up a great part of their working lives. With a top wage of 9*d* or 10*d* a day we would not expect them to make a fortune and the four labourers whose inventories have been studied all left goods amounting to less than £25. Robert Stevens, who left £21, held a lease of his house which was worth £5. He also had £5 owing him which he may have lent out at interest. He owned pigs, a ewe and a lamb, but their worth only amounted to 2 per cent of his goods. On the other hand, Thomas Ballamy, who left £11, had 68 per cent of his goods in livestock including his horse, worth £7. Like the craftsmen, the two labourers who owned less than £4 worth of goods had no livestock or leases and their only assets, apart from household goods and clothes, were their tools, valued at 12*s* and 6*s* 8*d*.

Although it can be no surprise to learn that labourers were not among the wealthier members of Stratford society, the fact that there are also six yeomen among the workers on the land who left less than £50 worth of goods may need some explanation, in view of the assertion that a yeoman was a successful husbandman. Five of these less wealthy yeomen were old by sixteenth-century standards and no longer had the livestock and cereals which were the main source of wealth with younger yeomen. Edward Ingram, for instance, who died in 1614 leaving goods worth £38, had his first child in 1558. If we assume that he married when he was twenty-six, which was the average age for a first marriage in Stratford, he would have been eighty-two when he died – a ripe old age when the average life span was forty-seven years. He owned no farm stock at the time of his death. It had probably all been passed to his sons. He did have the lease of a tenement in Stratford which, according to the appraisers, was worth £12. At least two of the other yeomen owned the houses in which they lived as well as other tenements which they let. None of these assets are included in their inventories. They were in a more advantageous financial position than at first appears.

The only one of the six yeomen who still held a considerable amount of livestock (15 per cent of his total wealth) and who does not seem to have been old at the time of his death, is Edward Wakeland. He married in 1622, his son John was born the following year and Edward died six years later. Although referred to as 'yeoman', he does not seem to have been a pillar of the community. According to the churchwardens' presentments he was a common swearer and blasphemer and, even after his marriage, was famed for incontinency with more than one woman.[21] It can only be speculation, but perhaps he followed his father into farming and then let things slide.

A more predictable scenario is to be found in the eight land-workers who left more than £95-worth of goods. Six of these were yeomen and the other two were very successful husbandmen, one of whom might very well have thought of himself as a yeoman although the friends and neighbours who compiled the inventory did not share his opinion. This was Richard Barbur of Drayton who left £98, half of which was in farm stock. His father, also Richard, who had died twenty years earlier, had referred to himself, in his will, as 'yeoman', although his inventory gives no indication of his status. His son Richard's will is not extant. The two inventories, twenty years apart and containing in many instances the same items, give an indication of the inflation which took place at the end of the sixteenth century since father Richard's goods totalled £69.

The other wealthy husbandman is Robert Munmore of Shottery. In his will, made in 1618, he refers to himself as husbandman. His inventory, however, totals £378, a very large sum for Stratford, the second highest amount of all the inventories. But £200 of this was in debts which were owed to him, and we have no way of knowing whether they were all recoverable. A large proportion of the rest of his wealth was in farm stock and it may have been that he acquired this through his marriage in 1597 to Mary Richardson, widow of John, a yeoman, who had died in 1594. We do not have John's will, only his inventory totalling £87. Robert and Mary had no children and in his will Robert left his stepdaughter, Margaret Richardson, £100 and his stepson, William, who was then thirty-seven, £10. Their mother, Mary, was residuary legatee and it seems likely that she handed over the farm to her son, for six years later, a William Richardson of Shottery died leaving £153 in goods, 70 per cent of them being farm stock.

William, then, was one of the five yeomen who died leaving goods worth over £100. Two others also owned farm stock and cereals which were worth a large proportion of the total. The sources of the wealth of the other two, however, are not so evident from their inventories. John Sadler senior, who lived in the town, in Church Street, was a miller as well as a yeoman. He owned the house he lived in as well as several others which he leased out. He also held the lease of the town mills and fishing rights. None of these are mentioned in his inventory where the goods total £177, 17 per cent of this being in agricultural goods and £36 in malt. One of the most influential men of the town, he died in 1583.

Richard Whiting, who died in 1628, when he was in his fifties, also lived within the town, where he owned a house in Bridge Street which he left to his wife in his will. He was the wealthiest of all the yeomen whose inventories survive. The total came to £209, but £110 of this was in debts due to him, and in ready money. He also owned twenty quarters of malt valued at £20. He had probably lost interest in maintaining farm stock since there was no one to inherit it, his son John having died four years earlier. The money he obtained from the sale may well have been lent out at interest.

The main sources of all the other yeomen's wealth were cereals and animals, and the later in the period under review that they lived, the more their stock became worth. From the inventories we can see the changes in value over the years. The price of barley which was the main cereal used for bread in Stratford, as well as being a necessity for the malt trade, was 13*s* 4*d* a quarter in 1574. In the middle of the 1590s the price rose to 26*s* 8*d* a quarter due to dearth. It had dropped to 18*s* by 1600 but steadily rose, then leapt to about 24*s* in 1625 following another period of dearth in 1622/3. This pattern is, of course, reflected in the price of malt which rose from 10*s* and 12*s* a quarter in 1583 to 20*s* in 1628.

The prices for livestock show a similar trend, although the quality of the beasts must also have been taken into consideration. Cows were worth between 20*s* and 30*s* in the 1580s, 40*s* in 1597, 20*s* again by 1600; but by 1627 the prices ranged from £2 3*s* 6*d* to £3 3*s* 4*d*. Sheep fetched 2*s* 6*d* each at the beginning of the period and between 5*s* 9*d* and 8*s* 6*d* at the end. The price of pigs rose from 3*s* 9*d* each to 13*s* 4*d*.

With this inflation in the prices of what were, in fact, the ingredients of the staple diet, it is small wonder that husbandmen and yeomen were among the wealthier members of Stratford society. Those craftsmen and traders who held sufficient farm stock to feed their families and have a little surplus to sell also benefited. It was the craftsmen without livestock, who owned one pig, or two hens, who suffered, although even they were in a much happier financial position than the indigent poor who left no record of their belongings. By 1630 the Corporation was doing its best to help them. On 26 January 1631 it was resolved that £40 should be laid out to buy corn to sell at a reasonable price to the poor, the members of the company to stand any loss made.[22] Throughout the whole period the price of loaves had been kept to 4*d*, 2*d* and 1*d*, although we are not told their weight.[23] Perhaps it was found easier to regulate the weight than the price. In 1609 bakers were forbidden to make cakes for sale on pain of a 40*s* fine. The price of ale, too, had remained constant by decree of the bailiff and burgesses. Apart from 1597, when it went up to 4*d* a gallon, and 1600, when it was 3½*d*, it remained at 3*d* a gallon, and small beer was sold at 1*d* for two gallons throughout.

Those who kept bees were able to provide honey for their families and possibly for sale. This would be a great asset, for sugar was expensive and, like everything else, was getting more so. From the chamberlains' accounts we see that the price of a pound of sugar rose from 1s 4d in 1586 to 2s 6d in 1612. At that same date even the less expensive meat, such as capons or rabbits, could only have been a rare treat for some households since capons were 10d each and rabbits 6d – a day's wages for a labourer.

As well as food, clothing was another necessity and, with the price of material rising, new clothes were usually out of the question. In many of the wills clothing was handed on. In 1580 Richard Ballamy left various items of his clothing to his four brothers and his nephew. None of the items appear in his inventory and may well have been distributed before the inventory was taken. However, in a large proportion of the inventories, apparel is appraised. It is usually set down as 'his (or her) wearing apparel', although in some cases it is itemized and the information about clothing gained from these inventories will be discussed in the next chapter. The value of the apparel ranges from 3s 6d (Abraham Allaway, a painter, in 1624) to £15 (Alice Williams, widow, in 1622 – see appendix – and Thomas Dixon alias Waterman, innkeeper, in 1602). This latter inventory, transcribed and published by J.O. Halliwell, lists the clothes in detail.[24] The average value of a person's apparel in the inventories is 30s.

Those who could afford new clothes found the prices of

Bees provided honey for sweetening and beeswax for polish. Stalls of bees (beehives) were listed in six inventories.

material rising throughout the period. In 1585 broadcloth was being sold at between 3*s* and 6*s* a yard, but by 1613 it was 10*s* a yard. White cotton, which sold at 5*d* and 6*d* a yard in 1585, retailed at 1*s* a yard in 1613. The prices of the 1585 materials are taken from the extraordinary inventory of John Brown, woollen draper, one of the three tradesmen whose goods amounted to more than £100. His inventory lists the entire stock of his shop in detail – broadcloths, kerseys, baizes, cottons and friezes – totalling £46 0*s* 10*d*. It includes such items as:

> brode clothes.
> Item 4 yerdes & ½ of a sad new color at 6*s* & 8*d* the
> yerd   xxx*s*
> Item 5 yerdes & quarterne of horsefleshe color at
> 5*s*4*d* the yerd   xxvii*s*   iiii*d*
> carseyes
> Item 8 yerdes 3 quarters of harebrayne color at 2*s*
> the yerde   xvii*s*   iiii*d*

His total wealth, excluding his doubtful and desperate debts, amounted to £143, but when those debts are added on, the total becomes £501.

George Whateley, the other draper who owned goods worth more than £100, does not appear to have been in the same league. His wealth (in 1593) totalled £105, but, according to his will, he owned land at Beaudesert, close to Henley-in-Arden, where other members of his family still lived. He also owned tenements there, as well as renting the tenement in High Street, Stratford, which he left to his daughter, Katherine. He was, therefore, wealthier than at first appears. William Smith, mercer, the third trader in this group, left £165 in 1600. Much of his wealth came from agriculture. Farm stock made up 27 per cent of the total. He also had malt worth £10, and the lease of a house in Henley Street in which he lived was valued at £6 13s 4d.

Two of the traders in Table 4 were maltsters and the rest dealt in wool or cloth and include the pedlar, Avis Clark. There were two wooldrivers, the middlemen between the sheep farmers and those who made the cloth. Both the wooldrivers owned horses and pack saddles, but, whereas John Robins had two horses, two pack saddles, two packcloths, two maling cords and two wampties, altogether worth £3 15s 4d out of his total of £18, Ralph Shawe's inventory merely refers to a gelding and packcloth worth 40s. His wealth, totalling £61, included £7 for a tod of yarn, as well as twenty quarters of malt worth £10. It is clear from his will that his elder son, Julius (July), also a wooldriver, had already received a stock of money and wool. Ralph also owned his dwelling house in Henley Street. He died in 1592, only four years after John Robins, and appears to have been the more successful of the two.

The wealth, or lack of it, of the widows listed in Table 4, reflected, on the whole, the fortunes of their late husbands. In all but four cases the husband's occupation is known and in six cases his inventory is also extant. Among these are the inventories of William and Joyce Hobday who died in 1601 and 1602 respectively. William was the glover whose goods, amounting to £66, included various types of skins. Joyce's goods were valued at £64 and still included skins as well as some of the debts which had been owed to her husband. Joan Biddle, widow of Robert, shoemaker and victualler, continued to brew ale for a living. The value of the lease of the house in which she and her late husband had dwelt and where she continued to live, although not included in her husband's inventory, was calculated in her inventory as worth £8. There were eighteen years of the lease still to run at 8s per annum, so that it was valued at twenty times the rent. One of the wealthiest widows was Alice Williams whose goods were valued at £163 in 1622. Her late husband was Thomas Williams, gentleman, who had died nine years earlier, leaving her lands in both

Gloucestershire and Warwickshire.[25] These are not mentioned in Alice's inventory which did, however, include £40 in money and jewels.

At the other end of the scale, there were two widows who died in the almshouses. We know the husband of one of them – William Fletcher, tailor, who died in 1600. In 1604 'Widow Fletcher' was sharing a room with 'Widow Balis' by Anne ffluellyn's chamber over the almshouses, for which they paid an annual rent of 12d.[26] When she died in 1608, owning £4 worth of goods, her burial was entered in the register as that of 'Alice Fletcher vidua elemozena' (almswoman); by then she had moved down into the almshouses below.

The inventory of one more widow is of considerable interest. Anne Lloyd died in 1616. Her inventory lists her clothes in great detail and they are valued at over £12. Debts of almost £20 were owed to her. One item gives us a hint of her late husband's occupation. It reads, 'Item an Instrument for cherurgerie . . . iiii^s'. Her goods totalled £56 and, in her will, she left £10 to the churchwardens for various charitable purposes, and to her friends personal items, such as two white laced handkerchiefs to Mr Henry Smith who was bailiff that year, a black and white stomacher 'new wrought' and a white stomacher to his wife, and the ring which she wore on her thumb to Thomas Lucas, a relation. Her mother, Joan Lucas, was her executor and residuary legatee so it seems that she died young.

The inventories which come under the heading 'others' in Table 4 are those of members of the 'service' industries, and also of six gentlemen. Two of the gentlemen left less than £35 worth of goods, the other four more than £70. Leonard Kempson was a member of an old county family. He had settled in the town and his inventory includes musical instruments, books and a Bible, items which rarely appear in Stratford inventories. He may very well have owned land, but his total goods amounted to a mere £23. This is in contrast to John Gibbs, a gentleman who died the same year (1625) and left goods totalling £308. He was owed debts amounting to £52, had fifty-seven quarters of malt and barley worth £85, and a lease of a tenement in Rother Street and an orchard in Henley Lane which had thirty-seven years to run and for which he paid an annual rent of 20*s* valued at £60.

Three other men who left over £100 worth of goods were innkeepers. One, Thomas Dixon alias Waterman, was the man whose inventory detailed his wearing apparel. Another, Lewis Hiccox, was the tenant of part of the house in Henley Street now known as Shakespeare's Birthplace. The original lease had been granted to Hiccox by William Shakespeare after his father's death. An item in Hiccox's inventory, made in 1627, reads:

> one Chattel & lease of the houses in henlye street of the
> demise & grante of William Shakespeare, gent for lxiii
> yeares the time therein yet to come and unexpired worth   lxv*li*

The lease, then, was worth £65 and Hiccox also had agricultural stock which made up 37 per cent of his wealth. In fact, he is referred to in the inventory as 'yeoman' although in other documents he is 'innkeeper'. His total wealth amounted to £375. The third innkeeper, Robert Johnson, also lived in Henley Street.[27] He, too, had a connection with William Shakespeare. An item in his inventory reads:

> Item the lease of a barne that he holdeth of Mr Shaxper   xx*li*

An unusual inventory is that of Simon Hunt, schoolmaster, who died in 1598 and is referred to as 'late of Stratford upon Avon'. In fact he had been replaced as schoolmaster in 1575 after four years at the free school. The only items in the inventory are three debts due under specialty, amounting to £50. Both the appraisers came from Newell in Worcestershire and it seems likely that Hunt settled there after leaving Stratford.

Shakespeare's Birthplace, Henley Street. This was the home of John and Mary Shakespeare, where John plied his trade of glover.

The existence of debts is one of two items which keep recurring in this discussion of the contents of inventories. The other is the value of any leases held. The valuation of leases will be discussed in Chapter Three, but the position with regard to lending and borrowing needs to be clarified. Usury was legalized in 1571 with a limit of 10 per cent interest, and any surplus capital could be made to work in this way. However, a list of debts owed to the testator in an inventory did not necessarily mean that money had been lent at interest. A debt in Stratford fell into one of three categories. Small loans between neighbours, friends and members of the family promoted goodwill and interest was seldom charged. The second category is of debts due for goods or services. Only twenty inventories mention cash and it was due to a shortage of coin that such credit was widely used. The third category is of money lent upon specialty or bond and it was then that interest was charged. Of the forty-seven inventories which list debts, only eight come under this last category. Of the inventories which do not list debts, twenty-four have accompanying wills which do and, of these, only two clearly relate to money lent at interest, and the same applies to three of the fourteen wills which mention debts and have no accompanying inventories.

An example of one of those inventories where debts due to the testator are listed in the will but not in the inventory is that of John Robins, wooldriver.[28] Although his inventory totals £18, from his will we learn that Richard Wattes of Yewemill in Gloucestershire, a clothier, owed him £62 19s – £40 by specialty. Edward Courte late of Stratford owed him £2 'which I lent him out of my purse' (a goodwill gesture?) and Richard Edwards of Hampton, Worcestershire, owed £4 6s 8d. The will also states that, 'The debtes I owe are all upon specialtie saving six poundes which I owe ferdinando Morris.'

John Combe, gentleman, of Old Stratford, was noted as a usurer and in his will he stipulated that every debtor should have 20s for every £20 he owed, and that Thomas Reynolds of Stratford, a personal friend, should be forgiven his debts and also receive a team of oxen with wagons and tumbrils, or forty marks. Lending and borrowing money at interest was common among the 'gentlemen born' of Stratford. Antony Nash of Welcombe, gentleman, was constantly taking people to court in order to recover money lent under bond.[29]

Humphrey Brace, a mercer, who owed over £300 to grocers and mercers of London as well as to Mr John Combe and Mr Nicholas Lane of Stratford, made it clear in his will how these debts were to be settled.[30] He was owed £180 by his 'man' Francis, and £67 by a Mr Bartlett. When these debts were settled the money was to be used to pay off some of his own debts. He was also owed money by those to whom he had given credit for goods and these were detailed in his debt book. As his wife, Elizabeth, his executrix, received the repayments each quarter, she was to discharge the rest of his debts and only then

The inventory of Margaret Smyth, widow, 1625. Born Margaret Sadler, she married John Smyth, vintner, in 1572. He died in 1601 and Margaret remained a widow for twenty-four years and was probably over seventy when she died. She was one of the twenty-five women in this study who could sign their names. Her signature appears on her will which was made less than a week before she died. A list of 'desperate' debts owing to her appears at the end of the inventory.

was she to pay out the legacies he had made in his will. If there was any loss the legatees were to bear it equally, but they were also to share any surplus. This is the only will in which such detailed instructions were given to the executrix and it would be interesting to know whether such arrangements were normal practice.

Lending money at interest as a way of increasing income was, of course, only feasible if there was surplus capital. Indeed, the other ways of supplementing income, malt-making or husbandry, also required initial outlay. The craftsmen who were able to benefit in this way were, presumably, able to make a reasonable living, but those who had to rely solely on their craft were at a disadvantage. Unskilled labourers suffered even more. Yeomen and husbandmen with adequate stock and arable land were able to benefit from the rise in prices, as were the woollen merchants. Gentlemen with spare capital and innkeepers who kept the larger inns were also in an advantageous position. In sixteenth- and seventeenth-century Stratford the gap between the poor and the comfortably off was a wide one.

CHAPTER THREE

GOODS, CATTLE AND CHATTELS

Living as we do in a consumer society, we find it hard to visualize the paucity of goods owned by even the most affluent of sixteenth-century Stratford townsfolk, or the loving care with which they bequeathed those possessions. Clothes, bed linen and cooking utensils figure alongside sums of money and items of furniture in many wills. Grace Amsden, a widow, who made her will in 1627, stipulated that her daughter, Ann, should receive £5, a trunk, three pairs of sheets, four napkins, her high bedstead, a towel, a feather bed, bolster and pillow, two pillowbears (cases), a dough kever, half of her nineteen pieces of pewter and her dozen spoons, her biggest kettle save one, a little pot, a gallon kettle, a dabnet, a chair, her lesser spinning wheel and a frying pan, her old gown 'that is pulled to pieces', her best red petticoat and hat, one tablecloth, two smocks, one white apron, a waistcoat and half of the rest of her petticoats. Another daughter, Grace, who was nominated her executrix, was treated in a similar fashion, except for the £5. Christian, her married daughter, received a lesser portion of household goods and her son, Lawrence, still an apprentice, had £5, a silver spoon, her great coffer and a posnet. Every one of these items is listed in her inventory, their value amounting to £32. Similar articles, in larger or smaller quantities, appear in a great proportion of the 168 inventories, although, in some cases, essentials such as apparel are omitted and others include farm stock, leases, debts and an occasional unusual item such as a picture or tobacco.

Wills were usually made a few days before death and inventories were compiled shortly after the funeral, so that, when items bequeathed do not appear in the inventory, doubts arise as to the completeness of the list of goods and chattels. Just occasionally the making of the will and inventory are months or even years apart and, in one or two cases, the makers of the inventory specifically state that such and such an item has been bequeathed. But these cases are rare and when goods which are known to have existed are absent from the inventory, then the omission can only be put down to human error.

This discrepancy exists in the case of Richard Ballamy's clothes, bequeathed in his will but not included in his inventory, and other examples include that of William Hobday who made his will on 15 December 1601 and left his rapier and dagger to a Bartholomew Parsons, although no weapons appear in the inventory made two weeks later. There are no weapons listed in William Smarte's inventory either, although he had bequeathed his sword and dagger to his brother-in-law, John Wells.[1] But these are minor discrepancies. When leases were not valued in the inventory, the difference in the total could be quite substantial. Valuations of leases range from £60 to 5*s*, depending, of course, on the number of years remaining of the lease and, also, the rent paid. William Toms, tailor, stated in his will that a certain Thomas Barlow granted him a lease of his dwelling house in 1596 for ninety years. When Toms died in 1622 his lease, with sixty-four more years to run, was valued in the inventory at £11 13*s* 4*d*. However, William Rogers, sergeant at mace, was granted a forty-one-year lease of his house in 1595 at an annual rent of 10*s*. He died a year later, but there is no mention of the lease in his inventory. With forty years still to run, a valuation of at least £5 might have been appropriate, bringing the total value of his goods up to £37. Thomas Alegh, a shepherd, whose inventory totalled only £2, held a lease with seven more years to run at a yearly rent of 12*s*. Even if this had been judged worth only 5*s*, it would have made a considerable difference to the total of his goods. Although any statistics in this chapter must perforce be based only on the items listed in the inventories, it is as well to keep such discrepancies in mind.

One item which everyone must have owned was his or her wearing apparel, although twenty-six inventories do not list any. The average

Shrieve's House, Sheep Street. In 1596 the house comprised a hall, a parlour, a kitchen, buttery and tavern, four chambers and two solars. After being partly destroyed by fire in 1594, it was rebuilt by the occupier, William Rogers, mercer and sergeant-at-mace, who was granted a new lease by the Corporation in 1595, for forty-one years at a yearly rental of 10s.

Compared with those of Elizabethan gentlemen, the clothes of countrymen and of craftsmen and traders in small towns such as Stratford were both practical and hardwearing.

value of a testator's clothing is 30*s*, although Alice Williams, widow, owned £15 worth out of her total of £163 (9 per cent), while wheelwright John Ashwell's clothing amounted to 4*s* out of a total of only £2 (10 per cent). In painter Abraham Allaway's inventory his clothes are valued at only 3*s* 6*d* out of £5 and that sum includes his purse and girdle. However, his wife's apparel is also listed. She had died one month before her husband. Her clothes consisted of '7 partletes, 2 carchowes, 1 quife, 3 aparnes, 1 crescloth, 2 ringes, one of brase the other sillfer, 1 silke gerdell', together with 'all the apre ware' valued at 5*s*, and '1 gounde too hates' also worth 5*s*.

Eleven inventories itemize the apparel and these present a fascinating insight into both men's and women's wear. In 1615 Thomas Mylls, the younger, owned two hats, three shirts, one doublet, two jerkins, three pairs of breeches, three pairs of stockings, eight bands, one pair of shoes and a pair of boots, while, in 1593, George Whateley, an alderman, owned two gowns, a chamlett jacket, two coats, one cloak and a doublet of damask.

Undoubtedly the most comprehensive list of women's clothing is that of Ann Lloyd, the surgeon's widow, who died in 1616. The items in the inventory referring to her clothing are here quoted in full:

Imprimis in the Deske one wastcote	v*s*
Item one velvet cape & old taffatie and lase	vi*s*
Item one smock skyrte	xviii*d*
Item a wastcote	xii*d*
Item one Crossecloth and other lynnens	xii*d*
Item one pair of silke garters	xvi*d*

Item in a lyttle box one aporn one lyttle tablecloth one neccloth foure pynners three Ruffes	xii^s	4^d
Item one handkerchef & other thinges in it	ii^s	
Item a pursse gerdle & knife		vi^d
Item in a nother box one wrought capp	iii^s	4^d
Item two pair of gloves	ii^s	
Item a maske & tiffanie		xviii^d
Item 2 scarffes	vi^s	8^d
Item two stomachers	vi^s	
Item one peare of cuffes	ii^s	
Item three Aporns	viii^s	
Item two shirtes & one smocke	xiii^s	4^d
Item two handkerchefes one pair of Couffes and other ymplementes	iiii^s	4^d
Item one Ruffe	vi^s	
Item one silke gerdle & a pair of gloves	v^s	
Item 2 paire of stokinges	v^s	
Item one kertle & skyrtes to it	vi^s	
Item a black Aporn	iii^s	
Item two other Apornes	iiii^s	
Item one grogram gowne	xl^s	
Item one stomacher & necloth	iii^s	
Item 2 hattes & three hatt bondes	xx^s	

Item two gownes & two pettcootes	iii^l	
Item one guilt ringe		xviii^d

In her Trunck

Inprimis fowr gould ringes	26^s	8^d
Item in silver & gould	v^l	xv^s

No other inventory has nearly so comprehensive a list. The only items of women's clothing not found there are a riding cloak and a safeguard. Both these occur in the inventory of Ann Shaw, widow

(1630) and a 'safegard' is listed in that of Elizabeth Hancocke, spinster (1619) (see Appendix). It is interesting to note that Ann Lloyd's inventory was compiled by two men, although one cannot help thinking that they were aided by Joan Lucas, Ann's mother.

It was not only women who were anxious that their clothing should be of use to their heirs. Avery Fullwood, gentleman, left to his son, Avery, a green coat, his canvas doublet, his 'worser' jerkin and breeches, his 'worser' hat and pair of stockings, one of his best shirts and a pair of shoes, and to his son John, his best jerkin, breeches and hat, two of his 'worser' shirts and a pair of shoes. In his inventory his wearing apparel was valued at £5 out of a total of £31.

An overskirt, called a safegard, protected the skirt from mud and dust and also gave extra warmth. In this picture the rider is also wearing a ruff, stomacher, cuffs and a wide-brimmed hat with a hatband – all articles listed in Ann Lloyd's inventory.

The inventory of Avery Fullwood, gentleman, who died in 1631. His apparel is valued at £5.
In his will the clothes were itemized and divided between two of his sons. (See page 60.)

In her trunk Ann Lloyd kept four gold rings. She also owned silver and gold (five pounds in weight) and a gilt ring. Gold was a rare commodity in Stratford and those who owned jewellery and silver were usually the wealthier sort, although this was not always the case. Abraham Allaway's wife, as we have seen, owned two rings, one of brass and one of silver, which were included among her husband's goods which totalled only £5. Margaret Smyth, widow (total goods £17), wore a ring on her finger worth 2*s* and out of Elizabeth Nott's total of £15 she owned a pair of silver hooks (probably dress fasteners), a silver spoon and a gilt ring worth 10*s*. Apart from the silver spoons which appear in many inventories, only nine list jewels or other objects of precious metal. There are also three wills without inventories where rings or plate were bequeathed, although in many other wills money was left to friends to buy rings. John Sadler the elder, yeoman and miller, owned silver salts, spoons and other pieces valued, in 1583, at just over £25. Much of this was left to his son, John.[2] When this John's widow, Isabel, died in 1627, she left a silver nut bowl to her granddaughter Elizabeth and a gold ring and a silver sugar bowl to another granddaughter, Isabel. Both William Smyth, linen draper (1578), and Thomas Williams, gentleman (1613), left 'jewels and plate' to their wives.[3]

Twenty-one of the inventories refer to cash or ready money. Most of these were of testators who died in the 1620s. Only two are sixteenth-century inventories, and this is possibly due to the fact that, at that time, there was a shortage of coin. The inventory of Clement Swallow, gentleman (1571), refers to £41 15*s* 'in the hands of John Myddlemore', and William Rogers, sergeant-at-mace (1596), had just 2*s* 6*d*. The cash held in the 1620s ranged from £1 8*s* to £20, although Richard Whiting, yeoman, had £110 'in ready money with debtes good upon specialtie & divers debtes desperate'.

Only nine inventories and three wills mention weapons, a surprisingly small proportion of those surviving. Thomas Tayler,

John Combe, gentleman, left £5 to Sir Francis Smith, knight, 'to buy him a hawke'. An effigy of Sir Francis Smith is carved on his tomb in the church at Wootton Wawen, ten miles north of Stratford.

fuller (1587), owned a bow and eight arrows, and John Sadler the elder (1583) had a crossbow. The nine men who owned either a sword or a rapier, usually coupled with a dagger, came from all walks of life, and five of them did not aspire to the title of 'gentleman'. One of the four who did, however, was William Shakespeare who left his sword to Thomas Combe, nephew of William Combe whose plans to enclose land at Welcombe caused dismay to many. Thomas Dixon alias Waterman, innkeeper, owned, beside his sword, a buckler (a small shield), a skene (a dagger) and a pistol. Leonard Kempson, gentleman (1625), was the owner of the only other firearms mentioned – a calliver (a light musket) and a 'birding piece'. Another method of catching birds was used by Clement Swallow (1571) and Richard Barbur (1598). They had nets for larking and Barbur also had a sparrow net. Hawking was not a sport indulged in by the ordinary folk of Stratford, but, in his will, John Combe, gentleman, left £5 to Sir Francis Smith, knight, 'to buy him a hawke'. John Combe's circle of distinguished friends who were remembered in his will included Sir Henry Clare, Sir Richard Verney, Sir Henry Rainsford and Mr William Shakespeare, to whom he left £5.

Leonard Kempson was not just a sporting gentleman. He also enjoyed music, for his inventory contains 'one payre of virginalls vi Cushins two vialls one case one Citterne one Recorder & flute & musick books', valued at £1 10s 0d. The only other musical instrument mentioned in the inventories is Ann Lloyd's fiddle, with fiddle cloth. The hardworking, down-to-earth people of Stratford had little time or money for the finer things of life and the inventory of Lewis Hiccox, innkeeper (1627), was the only one to list pictures among his possessions. Unfortunately there is no description of them and they are valued together with furniture, cushions, curtains and bed linen, at £6. For their relaxation some townsfolk looked to tobacco, the inventories of both Richard Whiting, yeoman (1628), and Edward Wakeland, yeoman (1629), coupling it with hogsheads of beer. William

Tobacco was a luxury few in Stratford could afford. Here the sight of the head of the family smoking seems to be causing some consternation among the children.

Greenway, carrier (1601), had some 'verinshe' among other items which appear to be goods he was to transport. This was a superior type of tobacco named after a town in Venezuela whence it came. Mary Mills, widow (1624), also had two barrells of 'verinice'.

Apart from Clement Swallow's law books, reading matter is mentioned only three times in the sixteenth-century wills and inventories. In his will, Thomas Tayler, fuller (1587), left his 'book' to brother Robert, although no book is mentioned in the inventory. Thomas Asteley (1584) owned two books which were valued, together with a cruse and bellows, at 12*d*, and John Pattreket (1587) had a psalm book. However, in the seventeenth century, books are listed fourteen times. Apart from the Bible, the books in all but one of the inventories are not named. In his will, Daniel Baker left to Holy Trinity Church a book of Mr Greenham's works, which he stipulated was to be chained for safe keeping.[4] Dr John Hall, Shakespeare's son-in-law, in his nuncupative will of 1635, asked his son-in-law, Thomas Nash, to dispose of his books and his manuscripts as he thought fit.[5] However, a really comprehensive list of books appears in the inventory of John Marshall, curate of Bishopton (1607).[6] There are 168 books valued at amounts ranging from 1*d* to 6*s* 8*d*. There are books in Greek, Latin and English, many, as might be expected, on religious subjects – not all Protestant. Thomas More's *Apology* heads the list.[7] Erasmus is well represented, six books by him including *Enchiridion Militis Christiani* and the *Colloquia*.[8] Treatises by Luther and Bucer, books on mathematics, and works by Virgil, Terence and Ovid were to be found side by side with *The Good Huswives Closet*, *The Art of Anglinge* and *The Voiage of the Wandringe Knight*.[9] One item reads 'B. Babington on genesis (geven away bi will)' and, sure enough, in the will, we read 'to Francis Hiccoxe my kinsman, Babington on Genesis'.[10] John Marshall also gave his son, Richard, Martin Luther on the *First and Second Epistles of St Peter*, and willed that, when they reached the age of fourteen, his three sons were to have all his books which he had not otherwise bestowed and that they were to decide who was to have which books 'according to their interests'.

The foregoing were all personal possessions, but in many, although by no means all, inventories, the bulk of the items are household goods – furniture, linen and utensils. Arguably the most important items of furniture are the beds. These were of varying types, the grandest being the standing bed, so named because it stood out into the room. These were normally made by a joiner and most had testers of cloth or wainscot and curtains. There was also the half-headed bed with just a headboard. Truckle beds could be pushed under the standing bed during the day. Bedsteads (or bedstocks as they were known in other parts of the country) were the simplest type of bed, made up of four lengths of wood with a leg at each corner and cord or webbing

A half-headed bedstead. The cord threaded across the frame was to support the mattress.

threaded across to support the rush mat and/or the straw mattress. Only one inventory, that of John Marshall, mentions a wall bed. Although the practice was becoming rarer, some people slept on a mattress or flock bed on the floor or a bench and this may well have been the case with some of the fourteen of the twenty-four testators whose inventories do not mention bedsteads at all, although they list bedding and some other furniture. Another reason could be that a standing bed was a fixture in the chamber and therefore not counted among the goods and chattels of the testator. Of the other ten inventories which do not list bedsteads, some mention only debts and apparel, and others farm stock and apparel, and it seems possible that the testators lodged with another family or, particularly in the case of the shepherds or labourers, with their masters. Avis Clark, the pedlar, owned an old pair of sheets and a blanket, but no bed or other bedding, and possibly lodged at various places on her travels.

Among those who, seemingly, had no bedsteads, we find William Cootes, skinner (1597), who owned three flock beds. At the time of his death he had three young daughters, and his accommodation appears to have consisted of one room and a buttery. In spite of the fact that one of his daughters was a small baby, no cradle is listed. Only seven inventories mention cradles and six of these are of fathers who died young leaving widows with very young infants. Another testator without a bedstead was Elizabeth Prettie (1604), widow of a butcher, who did, however, have a feather bed and a quantity of bed linen, a table, chair, stool and a pair of playing tables. Even when there were bedsteads in the house some servants did not warrant such luxuries. Katherine Salisbury (1591), widow of an affluent yeoman, had a

A sixteenth-century green-glazed chamber pot. Mentioned in twenty-one inventories, chamber pots were usually listed among the kitchen utensils.

bedstead and truckle bed in her own chamber and a standing bed in the guest chamber, but the maid's chamber contained just a flock bed with a blanket and covering. However, the coarse wool bed which William Adams, a tailor, owned was one 'that a poor man lyeth on'.

Most of those inventories which listed no bedsteads were made in the sixteenth century. In contrast, the incidence of standing joined beds increased as time went on. In the 1570s only 12.5 per cent of the inventories list one. By 1610 52 per cent list at least one and often more. But the amount of bedding remained constant throughout the period. Feather, flock or wool beds were placed on the mat or mattress or else used as a cover, much as a duvet is today. Sheets were flaxen, hempen or hurden, and feather or flock bolsters outnumbered pillows. For warmth there were wool blankets and other coverings, including twillies and hillings or coverlets of tapestry, dornix, saye, orris or thrum. While some people owned only one pair of sheets, a bolster and a blanket, others had a vast amount of bed linen. John Sadler the elder, with seven beds in his house, owned sixty pairs of sheets, four feather beds and ten flock beds, eleven bolsters, eight pillows with nine pairs of pillowbears, eight blankets and eight coverings. His linen press also contained nine and a half dozen napkins and twenty-four table cloths, but no towels. Although most people owned table napkins, essentials since there was no cutlery, towels were not so widely used. Those who owned them might have three or four although innkeepers Arthur Newell (1591), Francis Hill (1626) and Robert Johnson (1611) had twelve, seventeen and twenty-three respectively.

Apart from beds and presses, chests and coffers, little other furniture was to be found in the bed chambers. Five close stools are listed, one belonging to John Brown, woollen draper, who died in 1586, and the other three being in use in the early seventeenth century. The chamber pots, which appear in twenty-one inventories, and the sixteen warming pans, are usually listed under kitchen utensils.

After a place to sleep, a place to eat was a necessity. In the hall it was

A simple table board with trestles. This could be dismantled after use and stored against the wall.

usual to find a table board. This was a table top which would be supported on trestles. The table could be dismantled after use and stored against the wall. Most households owned one or two of these. The joined table, fixed to a frame, which was first introduced in the middle of the sixteenth century, was a much rarer piece of furniture in Stratford. Only nine are listed in the inventories, the earliest being that of Humfrey Plymley, draper, who died in 1594. To eat, the family sat on forms or stools, although the master of the house might well have a chair. Of the inventories, 119 list chairs, normally not more than two, although Robert Johnson, innkeeper (1611), owned thirteen. There is no description of the types of chair except in the case of William Smith, mercer (1600), whose chair was of wicker. This same chair appears in the inventory of William Smith's son, also William, in 1626, when it is described as 'twiggen'. Three inventories list a child's chair. There were settles to relax on after

A family at a meal, showing the simple table and stools. Children often remained standing while their parents sat.

the meal, their hard surfaces softened by cushions which appear in the majority of inventories. In some cases there were two or three, but many had a dozen or more. George Whateley, draper (1593), had twelve of downey and another six. Robert Johnson (1611) had forty in his inn. The materials used are sometimes specified – turkey, dornix, silk, orris and neeld. The most unusual were those belonging to David Ainge, butcher (1630), made of calfskin.

The walls were hung with painted cloths which figure in seventy-seven inventories, mostly in the sixteenth century. By the 1620s, only five of the thirty-three inventories list them. Wainscot, which replaced the cloths in the seventeenth century, may well have graced some of the walls in Stratford but, if it was a fixture, it would not have been listed in the inventories. It was, however, mentioned in nineteen, usually as 'a small piece of wainscot' and always in the hall. Portals, which could be either partitions fixed in front of doors to keep out the draught, or wooden screens placed between door and fire, are listed in eleven of the inventories from the 1590s onwards.

The joined stool was a common feature in sixteenth- and seventeenth-century homes. Several can be seen in the drawing of Lewis Hiccox's tavern on p. xx.

Something which one might reasonably expect to have been a fixture was window glass. However, thirteen inventories value the glass and it is, therefore, classed as moveable. This is confirmed in a will made by Alice Smyth, widow of William Smyth, linen draper, in 1584.[11] In it she stipulates that, if her eldest son William would let the new house to his brother, John, at a reasonable rent, then William should have all the window glass and wainscot. If not, the glass was to be sold by the executors and the proceeds were to be divided between the rest of her children. The inclusion of window glass in the inventories starts in the 1590s, although clearly it had been in Alice Smyth's new house in the '80s. But after 1610 it is valued as a moveable in only two inventories, presumably because it was now regarded as a fixture. Window curtains also begin to appear in the 1590s and nine inventories list them.

Apart from the ubiquitous chests and coffers, the hall and the parlour occasionally contained small tables of various shapes. One inventory refers to a round folding table and another to a little folding table. Two more inventories list pairs of playing tables. In 1630 we read of a long drawing table – an extending table, with the end leaves sliding under the middle section when the table was not in use. In 1606 an inventory lists 'a dresser', which was a table for dressing meat and other foods and not the 'cupboard' with shelves above which we know as a dresser today. The hall, however, usually contained at least one 'cupboard'. This could be a side table or just open shelves on which to display the pewter, although, after 1610, we begin to read of court cupboards – still consisting of open shelving, but usually in three tiers and with a drawer under the middle shelf. In 1593, another inventory lists a cupboard with a desk over it. Ann Lloyd owned a desk in which she kept a waistcoat, so 'desk' did not necessarily mean a writing table. John Marshall's desk had a lock, key and hinges and was worth 20*d*. He was the curate who owned the large number of books and his may very well have been for writing. Other cupboards are described as 'a standing cupboard', 'a joined cupboard with a head to it', 'a glass cupboard' (to display glass), and 'a joined cupboard with a press'. There is also a lattice cupboard which is mentioned twice – in Arthur Boyce's inventory in 1593 and in his son Francis's inventory in 1617. This was a small cupboard with open-work wooden doors for storing bread.

The pewter which was displayed on the shelves appears, throughout the period, in almost all of the inventories which list household goods.

Left: A sixteenth-century pewter bell-based candlestick. Candles were normally made of tallow (animal fat) since wax candles were expensive. Tallow is listed in several of the inventories although only one, that of George Whateley, mentions a candle-mould. Right: A round, three-legged table. The hall and parlour often contained small tables of various shapes.

A rare sixteenth-century plain tester bed from Anne Hathaway's cottage.

Some inventories list only one item, but Humfrey Allen, shoemaker (1617), owned 'six score and three pounds' in weight of pewter and brass, worth £3 10s 0d. Leonard Kempson's £2 worth of pewter was made up of: 'viii platers xii small platers xii sallet dishes and sawcers five porringers one basen iiii candlesticks one Candlecupp one flagon iii small peeces of pewter viii spoones iii chamber potts.'

Candlesticks of brass are valued in several inventories together with brass pots, kettles, skillets, chafing dishes, skimmers and ladles. Like pewter, brass utensils were used throughout the period, although some people owned only one brass object. While pewter and brass were often proudly displayed in the hall, the everyday platters, which were either treen (wooden) or tin, were kept in the kitchen or buttery along with the cooking utensils, some of brass, but mostly of iron. Fire irons were to be found in most inventories in the hall as well as in the kitchen. The inventory of William Badger, glover, made in 1585, contains typical items of this sort. Some items are self-explanatory and others are glossed in the appendix.

In the halle . . .

Item a pere of Anndiornes a fyreshowle a pere of
   tonges twoo haninges for a potte & a pere of
   pothookes   iiii^d

Item six platters three sawcers on pewter pott
   foure saltsellers price   v^s

In the butterye . . .

three barrelles twoo lomes on utinge fate twoo
   pales on stryke on whoppe   vi^s viii^d

Item xvii peces of pewter iiii sawcers iiii ketteles
   ii braches iii pottes on pere of cobberds on
   fryenge panne on chaffinge dyshe on trene
   platter iii crusses & a skymer   price   xxv^s viii^d

In the kytchen . . .

a cotherne twoo dabnettes a bolding wiche
   ii kyvers on troughe on barrell ii bagges a
   henpen & a gridyrne   x^s ii^d

All these utensils add up to £2 9s out of his total of £23.

A court cupboard on which pewter and other valuables such as plate could be displayed.

Thirty-seven years later much the same utensils were being used but were costing more, unlike furniture, which does not seem to have increased in price. The following is an excerpt from the inventory of Richard Baker, woollen draper, made in 1622:

Inprimis in the hall . . .
Item 2 dozen of pewter sorted xx sallet
   dishes & plates viii porringers fower
   candlesticks 3 Duble salts, i beaker
   i Candlecup, i brasse sconce 4 sawcers
   xvi spones   ii^{l} ii^{s}
Item in the kitchin
4 Brasse potts 4 kettles ii dabnits, ii posnits
   i brasse chafing dish, i warming pan,

A wall cupboard used for displaying dishes, plates etc.

ii brasse candlesticks, i flagon, 8 platters,		
vi sawcers candlestick, i old salt	ii^l	xiii^d
fower spitts, ii paire of lincks, i pair of		
pothooks, i paire tongs, i fyer shovel,		
vi peeces of Tin plate, i little chair & a little		
table & other Ymplements, ii Tyn dripping		
pans i smoothing iron	xii^s	
Item in the backsyde		
i Ewting fatt, i herecloth, i trye & i brewing		
lome	ilvi^s	viii^d

In spite of the fact that this list includes one or two extra items, the total cost of the utensils, £6 13*s* 8*d* out of his total of £35, is a substantial increase over the value of William Badger's goods. Apart from spoons, there is no mention of cutlery in any of the inventories with the exception of that of Francis Hill, innkeeper (1626), who owned two fleshforks. Another item which only appears once is a candle mould, although several inventories list tallow. The mould was owned by George Whateley (1593).

The existence in thirty-eight of the households of yewting or uting vats, which held the barley when it was soaking, points to the prevalence of malt-making. Many more inventories listed the wherewithal to brew ale, together with a quantity of malt. This activity was usually carried out in one of the outhouses in the backside. If the backside also contained a well, the 'furniture' (the kerb, pail and chain) was valued in the inventory.

Outhouses could be the householder's place of work, as in the case of Robert Young, dyer (1595), who in his 'working house' had 'ii boylinge leades with their frame, on[e] culbe, ii great vates [vats] and a wad [woad] vate, ii gutters of wod [wood], a payer of scales . . . half c waight of lead, a skypp and a jacke for the wad vate'. Many more craftsmen kept their tools in the house or the adjacent shop. Richard Homes, weaver (1593), kept his looms in his shop. Besides a pair of looms, two kersey looms and a bastard loom, there were two warping bars and two troughs which, together with a chair and 'odd stuffe', were valued at 30s 4d. His son, William, who had died three years earlier, kept his 'one weving loom with the gears thereto belonging' in his loft. A weaver of haircloth, John Pattreket (1587), had 'one frame caled a tente wythe the treyseyles that ys to ytt one whele & serten pattenes off olde papers i letell stole & serten brokes i pere of yerene blades & the stoke to them to wynde yerne wythe.' These were priced at 5s, but in a second copy of the inventory we find the following note: 'all thes longe to the occpacyon off heares workers gyven by Mr Wyllm Shylden decessed & so to Remayne for ever yett we have pressed them here in this envetory before we dyd knowe the truthe therfore conseder off ytt.' In spite of the erratic spelling, it is clear that the tools Pattreket worked with were not his own.

The inventory of Richard Ballamy, referred to as a locksmith (1580), shows that he also worked as a general smith.

In primis in the shoppe one payr of balles
Item one anfyle one vice one bychorne
Item one forehammer to hand hammers
Item one naylynge hammer iiii payr of tonges
Item one payr of plyars one locke saw
Item to buttris one brest wymble and a gimlet
Item to payr of pynsonnes to shuenge hammers
Item to studes xx^{ti} fyles v prechels
Item one yerne doge ii nayles toles
Item iii horse lockes one halter
Item one Revetynge hamer one hachett
Item one grenddlestone one fyre shule
Item one hurst stafe ii dosyn of shws
Item one payr of shepycke greires one stafe pycke
Item one stocke locke to chesselles one lanterne.

All these are valued at 20s. Although the use of some of the tools is unclear, it can be seen that Ballamy, although termed a locksmith, had all the equipment to shoe horses. Another unusual list of working tools is in the inventory of Robert Ingram, fisherman. In his kiln house he kept an old draughtnet, a boat, a bottom of a boat with two boards for the side, and six putchions (eel traps). The only other inventory to mention a draughtnet is that of John Sadler the elder, yeoman, who rented the fishing rights on the Avon.

Besides their tools the inventories of craftsmen also listed their stock-in-trade, as did those of several traders, particularly John Browne, woollen draper. The inventory of William Hobday, glover (1601), also has a comprehensive list of his stock:

Item all the made ware praysed at		xl^s	
Item ii hundred and ii dosen of sheps lether in the pytts at		xl^s	
Item xix of bucks lether in the pytts at		l^s	
Item xvi calves skyns in the pytts at		v^s	
Item ii horse hydes and one cow hyde in the pytts praysed at		vi^s	
Item ten dow skyns in the heare at		xiii^s	iiii^d
Item vi horse hydes redy drssed at		xiii^s	iiii^d
Item ii dosen of deres lether & xv Irish skyns at	iiii^l	iiii^s	
Item xiii dosen of calves lether redy dressed	iiii^l	xiii^s	iiii^d
Item an hundred and fowr dosen of sheps lether and an hundred and iiii dosen of lambes lether dressed at		xliiii^s	
Item v dosen and odd skyns of shepes lether that is tanned at		xx^s	
Item half an hundred of sheps lether in the Allam and viii dosen of lynyngs, wyth xvii doggskyns & other broken lether		xxviii^s	
Item all his woll both fyne and cowrse praysed at	x^l		

Two of the appraisers of this inventory were Robert Butler and John Cocks, both glovers. Their expertise was necessary to distinguish between the types of skins which were in varying stages of preparation. It is clearly stated when the items referred to are whole skins so that, assuming 'all the made ware' refers to the finished gloves, such statements as 'ii hundred and ii dosen of sheps lether' seems likely to mean 224 pieces of leather, valued at just over 2d a piece, which were of a size from which a pair of gloves could be fashioned. The cost of a finished pair of gloves would vary according to the material used and the workmanship. At the end of the inventory it is set down that a Mr Busshell of Broad Marston owed 4s 6d for gloves, although it does not say for how many pairs, but when Joyce Hobday, William's widow, died in 1602, John Edwards owed her 8d for two pairs of gloves. No will or inventory of John Shakespeare has been found, but his stock would have been similar to that of William Hobday, at least during the time of William's childhood, when John was a successful craftsman/trader.

The stock for yeomen and husbandmen was, of course, farm stock, although the inventories show that farmers were by no means the only owners of animals. Sheep, pigs, cows or oxen figure in eighty-four inventories. Of the thirty-five inventories of persons living outside the borough, thirty list livestock – often a considerable amount. Of these, twenty-five mention sheep, in several cases flocks of twenty or more. Nicholas Checket of Bridgetown (1572) had 160, valued, even at that date, at 3s each. Only nine town dwellers owned sheep. Many more owned pigs, which are listed in sixty-eight inventories, fifty of which were those of people who dwelt within the borough. Most households kept one or two, although Lewis Hiccox, innkeeper (1627), had 'twelve swine of all ages' valued at £5. Cattle, including oxen, figure in forty-two inventories, twenty-six from outside the borough. However, the most valuable collection was that of William Smith, mercer (1600), who lived in Henley Street. He owned eight oxen, nine kine and one bull and two heifers worth £48 13s 4d. Robert Munmore, husbandman, of Shottery (1618), had 'therteene kine some steers and some heiffers yere old and vantage and six weining calves the price £38'.

Horses were owned by thirty-nine of the testators. Some were clearly used in agriculture and the inventories list carts and tumbrels (two-wheeled carts). Richard Smart, husbandman, of Luddington (1571), owned ten horses and mares and an unspecified number of carts, with cart gear, altogether valued at £6 10s, while Thomas Hiccox, yeoman

Those living in the outlying hamlets who were fortunate enough to own or to be able to hire a horse, could convey goods to market in panniers such as these.

(1611), owned a horse, geldings, mares and colts numbering eight, worth £20. He also had two carts, two harrows and two ploughs. Although he originally came from Welcombe, he was living within the borough when he died. Five other townsmen owned harrows and ploughs as did thirteen of those outside the borough. Those with crops who did not own horses, carts, ploughs or harrows may very well have borrowed from their more fortunate neighbours. George Whateley owned a roan mare for riding. Complete with saddle and bridle, she was worth 40s. It seems that his daughter, Katherine, also rode, for in the inventory of his son-in-law, Thomas Kirby, the only saddle mentioned is a side saddle. Richard Whiting, yeoman (1628), and Robert Johnson, innkeeper (1611), owned saddles and a quantity of hay, but there are no horses listed in their inventories.

The thirty-nine people who owned poultry were most likely to have several hens and a cock; seven of them owned ducks as well. Those owning geese all lived outside the borough. Geese can be noisy neighbours. Poultry would provide eggs as well as meat for the table, although none of the inventories lists eggs. The food most frequently mentioned is bacon, some people having as many as six flitches hanging in their loft or in the kitchen. Ten also had beef, two listed in the inventories as 'plates' of beef and two others specifying 'Martlemas beef' (beef killed at Martinmas and salted for the winter). Cheeses occur in ten inventories and butter in three. Christopher Smith alias Court, yeoman (1586), was the only testator to have all these provisions. His inventory lists nine dozen cheeses, seven gallons of butter, half a beef and two flitches of bacon, altogether worth £3 6s 8d. Since sugar was expensive (no inventories include a sugar loaf), sweetening was provided by honey and six inventories list stalls of bees which would also provide beeswax for polish. Other

Cheeses are listed in ten inventories. Christopher Smith alias Court had nine dozen.

food stuffs occurring once or twice in the inventories are onions, garlic, apples, 'garden stuff', salt, bread and milk.

The prevalence of malt has already been mentioned. Barley was the most usual crop, either on the ground or in barns. Many inventories list some sort of cereal – barley, oats and wheat – as well as peas and beans. Flax and hemp were also grown and stored in the house. The amounts recorded in the inventories vary considerably. Thomas Hiccox of Welcombe, husbandman (1606), had, in his barn, a kench of wheat and a bay of barley worth £13 6s 8d, and two stacks and a kench of peas and beans worth £6 13s 4d. He also had fifty-seven lands of wheat and rye worth £19, and thirty-two lands ploughed for barley worth £3. In direct contrast we learn that John Ashwell, wheelwright (1583), had 'a little plecke of flax in the garden' worth 12d.

Although many of the goods mentioned in the inventories occur throughout the period, there were some items already in common use

Many town households kept pigs. Some were left to roam the streets and root among the rubbish.
Their owners risked incurring a fine, as did those who kept unauthorized muckheaps. In this
picture there are three in close proximity to the watercourse running through the street.

during the sixteenth century, at least in the south of England, which
the people of Stratford were slow to adopt and which only begin to
appear after 1600. William Harrison, writing about the 1570s and
referring to the 'old-fashioned' custom of sleeping on a mattress on
the floor, states 'it is not very much amended as yet in some parts of
Bedfordshire and elsewhere further off from our Southern parts'.[12]
The Midland town of Stratford was clearly on the wrong side of the
north-south divide, and still had not 'amended' its ways in 1600.
Harrison also refers to window glass as being plentiful, although in
Stratford it was still counted as a moveable in 1600. Other items
which do not appear until later than expected include tobacco, hops
(which are mentioned in only two inventories, although they had
been in use in England for a considerable time), wainscot in any
quantity, joined tables and standing beds. In those cases where the
inventories of two generations in one family are extant, it is possible
to trace the same items of furniture remaining in use throughout the
sixty years. Therefore it may not have been thought necessary or even

desirable to purchase more modern items, even if the wherewithal was available – an option, in any case, only for the more affluent families. In spite of the influx of visitors twice yearly at fair times, even after the turn of the century Stratford presents a picture of a community of conservative people, chary of trying new-fangled ideas and well content to live, for the most part, as their fathers and grandfathers had done.

CHAPTER FOUR

FAMILIES AND FRIENDS

The state of marriage was thought a desirable one, both for mutual comfort and support, and for raising children to carry on the family name, and young men of Stratford were expected to marry once they had completed their apprenticeship. Bachelors aged more than thirty were rare; so much so that the compilers of the 1595 list of maltsters felt it necessary to explain that John Page 'a smith by trade' was 'a man never married'.[1] At the time John Page was forty-seven years old and he died aged sixty-four, still unwed.

When seeking a bride the men of Stratford rarely looked farther afield than the outlying hamlets of the parish and, provided it was agreeable to the family, their choice usually seems to have been dictated by mutual attraction. Arranged marriages were only for the rich. Of course it was an advantage if the bride could bring goods or money to the marriage, and this she usually did, although, except in the cases of the most affluent families where land was concerned and marriage settlements were drawn up, the bride's contribution was normally some household goods and a small sum of money.

The dates are known of 393 marriages which were entered into by the subjects of this study. Most of these were solemnized at Holy Trinity Church and appear in its register. Some others took place at Alveston. However, twenty-eight have been traced to other parishes within the Midlands, and legend has it that William Shakespeare was married at Aston Cantlow, a few miles from Stratford. Several couples are known to have been married at Alcester, one or two at Warwick and five as far away as Mancetter and Kingsbury (both north-east of Birmingham) and Astley (north-west of Worcester). In the twenty-three cases where it was the bridegroom who came from Stratford, the couple returned and settled in the town. Of the five brides from

Stratford, four remained with their husbands in Birmingham, Wellesbourne or Warwick, but Elizabeth Biddle, who married Philip Bridges at Temple Grafton in 1619, returned with him to Stratford where their seven children were baptized and they were both buried. Of those marriages which took place outside Stratford, twenty-two occurred after 1600 (fourteen after 1610) suggesting that the tendency to look farther afield for a marriage partner increased after the turn of the century.

There is occasional evidence pointing to marriages outside the Midlands. Hamnet Sadler's sister, Jane, married Ralph Ridley of London although she was buried in Stratford. Daniel Baker, referring in his will to the settlement made when he married his third wife, Katharine, mentions his two brothers-in-law, each of whom had a different surname. John Waterhouse was 'late of Whitchurch, Buckinghamshire' and Thomas Spicer lived at Marston Pillage in Bedfordshire. The exact relationships here are not clear but it seems likely that Katharine Baker came from the Buckinghamshire/ Bedfordshire area. These, however, are isolated cases. Even when no record of the marriage can be traced, many of the wills provide evidence that the testator had married a local partner. A brother-in-law or father-in-law, appointed supervisor of the will, often proves to be a local man, although it is advisable to keep in mind the fact that the phrase 'in-law' could also be applied to a step-relation.

Remarriages were common, and especially desirable when young children were involved, although, of the 102 people in this study who married more than once, only nineteen widowers and five widows had young children at the time of the second marriage. These included Thomas Sharp, a tailor, who married first in 1561. His wife, Margaret, bore him two children who were aged four and one when she died in 1567. One year later Thomas married again. This second wife bore him no children, but was stepmother to young Isabella and Richard who were still only twelve and nine when she too died. Within seven months Thomas had married for the third time. He had two daughters and two sons by this marriage, although only one son survived infancy. This third wife died in 1582 when her surviving son was two years old. By this time Isabella and Richard were nineteen and sixteen and had, most likely, left home, but Thomas, left a widower for the third time, had two-year-old Charles to care for. Some time before 1589 he married his fourth wife, Elizabeth, who bore him one son. This infant too died young and his mother lived on until 1605, dying three years before her husband who had, therefore, been a widower four times.

Margaret Cootes was a widow who remarried. Her first husband, William, a skinner, died in 1597, leaving her with three small daughters, the eldest aged seven and the youngest, one. Baby Anna died one month after her father and just one more month elapsed before Margaret married Mr Richard Byfield, the vicar, whose first wife had died two months earlier. He already had a son, Nicholas, who was eighteen. Both Nicholas, and the son Margaret bore her second husband, became noted puritan divines.

Many appear to have married for a second or even a third time in the hope of having a family, or to comfort their declining years. Edward Wilkes, yeoman, may well have had both reasons in mind. He married first in 1594 but his wife, Frances, died eighteen years later. They had no children. Eight months after his wife's death Edward married Katherine who bore him a child in 1616. Both she and her baby died. Edward married for the third time in 1622 when he must have been about fifty and his bride was thirty-one, but Edward died six years later, still childless, and his widow, Ann, outlived him by ten years.

This same Edward was one of two testators whose wills contain the same unusual form of words when referring to their wives, the other being that of Robert Hollis, husbandman, whose will reads: 'I give and bequeath unto my wief with whom I copled myself in the fear of god refusinge all other Women the summe of twelve pence.' This rather forbidding way of describing a marriage partner may well have been a set formula used by whoever wrote the will, for both wills using this phrase were made in the 1620s. In the case of Edward Wilkes, he *did* name his wife, and made her his residuary legatee and executrix. Robert Hollis, on the other hand, made a relative his executor and left him the rest of his goods. He did not mention his (anonymous) wife again. True, he had little to leave, since his goods amounted to less than £3.

Antagonism can be read into wills where probably none exists, most famously in the case of William Shakespeare's second best bed. Nevertheless, Robert Hollis's will contrasts strongly with that of Thomas Hiccox, yeoman (1611), whose will reads:

> first for the kind affection which I beare unto my beloved wife, Elizabeth, and upon the confidence which I repose in her faithful and careful love which she will show unto me in the virtuous breeding of those children which are or shall be between us, I do testify hereby and my will is that she shall have and enjoy all and every of the houses, barns, stables, yards, gardens and all and singular edifices and buildings both free land and Chamber land set lying and being in Henley Street.[2]

Elizabeth Hiccox (née Sturley) was pregnant when her husband died. Lewis, her fifth son and sixth child, was born three months later, and Elizabeth, with six children under the age of eleven years, married Laurence Wheeler in 1612. She outlived him and several of her sons, dying in 1659 when she must have been about eighty. Like Ann Wilkes, she was her husband's executrix and residuary legatee. This was the normal arrangement between husbands and wives, surely signifying a degree of trust and mutual respect in most marriages.

It has proved possible to calculate the age at first marriage of 106 men. Of these, 74 per cent married between the ages of twenty and thirty, with the greatest number of marriages (fifteen) taking place when the bridegroom was twenty-four. This would have given him time to become settled in work after the expiry of his apprenticeship. However, the average age at first marriage was higher – twenty-six years – since far more men married for the first time between the ages of thirty and forty than before the age of twenty. In fact, only three married in their teens, the youngest being George Davis, a gardener, born in 1585. He married Margaret Batha a month after his seventeenth birthday. William Baylis, cooper, married Anne Russell when he was eighteen. Neither of these appear to be 'shotgun' marriages since William Baylis's first child was baptized twelve months after the wedding, and George and Margaret Davis had no children, unless, of course, Margaret had a miscarriage. The other eighteen-year-old bridegroom was William Shakespeare whose bride *was* pregnant at the time of the marriage. Although, as will be seen, pre-nuptial conception was not uncommon in Stratford, the youth of the bridegroom, particularly when compared with the age of his bride, made Shakespeare's marriage an unusual event which was doubtless a subject of comment among the townsfolk.

The ages of sixty brides at first marriage are known and here, although the average age was twenty-four, the favoured ages were either seventeen or twenty-one. The oldest of the sixty brides was forty-two. This was Margery Fullford, born in 1592, who married Richard Rogers, aged fifty-one, a widower, in 1634. His wife had died a year earlier. In 1639 at the age of forty-seven Margery died giving birth to a son, Richard, who survived. His father died of the plague six years later.

The youngest bride, Elizabeth Tibbots, was only twelve when she married William Parker, a widower, in 1628. However, their first child was not born until 1632 when Elizabeth was sixteen and it is possible that, although the marriage was solemnized, it was not consummated until later. This may also be what happened in the well-documented case of Katherine Whateley, who was born in 1584. A Corporation lease made in 1598 refers to Thomas Kirby, butcher, of Henley-in-Arden and Katherine his wife, daughter to George Whateley, late of Stratford-on-Avon deceased.[3] However, in the council minutes, the same lease is discussed and Katherine is referred to as Katherine Whateley, daughter of George Whateley. She is to agree to rebuild the house, damaged by fire, within six years 'after she is of full age'.[4] No record can be traced of her marriage to Kirby but the first of her children mentioned in the baptism register is Thomas, born in 1606 when Katherine was twenty-two. There was an older son George whose baptism was not registered in Stratford.[5] Thomas Kirby died in 1614 and, a year later, Katherine married William Deabank. We do not know when Thomas Kirby was born but it is likely that he was considerably older than his wife.

It has been possible to calculate the ages at death of ninety-eight males and sixty-three females over sixteen years of age, among the 800 Stratfordians and their families. Of the men, seventy-six were married and their ages at death ranged from thirty-one to eighty-three. John Bellamy, yeoman, who died aged thirty-one, left three children aged seven, five and four, to be brought up by their mother, Alice, who was pregnant when her husband died. The little boy, Benjamin, born five months later, died when he was seven months old. The 83-year-old was George Badger, draper, a recusant and a colourful character who had fathered sixteen children, fifteen of whom lived to adulthood – quite a record! The ages at death of the twenty-two single men lay between seventeen and thirty, except for John Page who died at sixty-four. Apart from a 'p' against the names of plague victims in the burial register, there is rarely any indication of the cause of death in younger men. We know that John Ingram, the nineteen-year-old son of Edward Ingram, yeoman, was drowned and that Richard Waterman's son, Thomas, was stabbed to death at the age of twenty-four, but other deaths must have been caused by illnesses which today may well have been treatable.

Table 5 shows that, while a considerable proportion of men (41 per cent) died between the ages of fifty and seventy, a large proportion of women (46 per cent) were between twenty and forty when they died. This was not, as might be imagined, due mainly to childbirth, since all those who died before they were thirty and over half of those who died between the ages of thirty and forty were unmarried.

Table 5. Age at death for men and women who reached adulthood between 1570 and 1630.

Age (years)	Men (%)	Women (%)
17–19	6.00	9.50
20–29	13.25	22.00
30–39	17.50	24.00
40–49	13.25	13.00
50–59	18.50	11.00
60–69	22.50	9.50
70–79	6.00	9.50
80+	3.00	1.50

Note: Figures are based on those 161 individuals who reached adulthood (ninety-eight men and sixty-three women), the dates of whose baptism and burial are both known.

Although among the families in this study twenty-one women died in childbed, the ages of only two of them are known. Margery Rogers, as has been seen, was forty-seven, and Frances, the first wife of John Samuel, ironmonger and sergeant-at-mace, was thirty-two. She died in March 1606 as did her baby, their first child after three years of marriage. We can only tell if the death was due to childbirth if the infant's baptism or burial is also recorded in the register. Other women may well have died after a miscarriage and, as the poorest families are not represented in this survey, this summary clearly does not convey a complete picture. The youngest of the thirty-two married women whose ages we know at death, was Elizabeth Hornby, aged thirty-one, who had three sons aged six, four and two. Complications in a fourth pregnancy may well have caused her death.

The oldest married woman was eighty-five when she died. Ann Woodward had been a widow for twenty-three years. The age range of deaths among single women was seventeen to fifty-nine. Among the seventeen-year-olds was Ann Reynolds, eldest daughter of William Reynolds, gentleman, who had sufficient worldly goods of her own to warrant her making a will, in which she left, among other legacies, all her clothes and jewels to her sister, Elinor, and £120 and a heifer to her mother (a widow) who was her executrix. Her inventory shows that she owned goods worth £148 and that she had been left property in Stratford and Shottery by her father who had died four years earlier. He also left her £110 and the heifer. The 59-year-old was Joyce Smart, daughter of William Smart, tailor, who was left small legacies in several wills and who was referred to as Joyce Smart, spinster, in the will of John Bellamy (1652). She died in 1677. Others who died unwed were Susannah Johnsons who died of plague aged twenty, and Mary Symson, 'the blind wench' who was admitted to the almshouses in 1596 when she was twenty-six, and died there five years later.

The incidence of deaths among children was very high: 32 per cent died before reaching the age of sixteen, 11 per cent before they were one month old, and 9 per cent within a week of birth. Where the register records the burial of unnamed infants it has been assumed that they were new-born.

Some families managed to overcome the ravages of unhygienic conditions, poor diet and disease and, like George Badger, raised large families of apparently healthy children. Six families had nine children who all lived to adulthood. Other families were bereaved time and time again. John Greene and his wife Margaret lost five of their six children, all as young babies. Ann, wife of Richard Sutton of Shottery, bore him ten children in the space of twenty years. Nine of them died, little Maria living the longest. She died aged four-and-a-half. Only her elder brother, Thomas, survived. Ann's last daughter, Thomason, lived for two weeks, and her death was followed by that of her mother a week later. Richard Sutton married again after two years when his surviving son, Thomas, was seventeen, but he had no more children.

Childish ailments, poor diet and childbed practices combined with general unhygienic conditions to produce this high incidence of infant mortality and people had no alternative but to accept the dreadful toll. Nathaniel Duppa must, however, have felt some helpless rage when, having raised a presumably healthy little boy, he drowned when he was six-and-a-half. However, Nathaniel already had another son and a daughter to comfort him and later five more children were born to him and his wife, Joseph being the only one not to reach adulthood.

The number of couples who consummated their marriage before the church gave its blessing cannot, of course, be calculated. It may well have been accepted that an espousal or promise to marry before witnesses, either in the present or future tense, sanctioned co-habitation.[6] Certainly, among the 393 marriages, at least fifty-four brides were pregnant at the time of the church ceremony. However, J.M. Martin quotes a figure of eighty instances of pre-nuptial conception out of a total of 266 marriages in the parish of Old Stratford between 1580 and 1624.[7] The discrepancy is probably accounted for by the fact that, while Martin included all marriages within those dates, the figures quoted here are confined to the people in this study, testators and their relatives and friends, and thus exclude the very poor. This would seem to suggest that, among the 'better sort' pre-nuptial conception was not so prevalent. It was not, however, confined to the 'lower orders'. Mr Henry Wilson, fishmonger and gentleman, three times bailiff, had no children by his first two wives but four years after the death of the second, he married Margery Mills who, four months after the ceremony, gave birth to a son who died. As we know, the young William Shakespeare, son of an alderman, also transgressed in this fashion. His daughter, Susannah, was born six months after her parents' wedding. Compared with these two instances, members of the Biddle family tended to practise brinkmanship. William Biddle, butcher, married Katheryn Wood on 2 February 1578 and their son, John, was born on the 25th of the same month. His kinsman, another William, sergeant-at-mace, married in June 1613 and had a son, Richard, the following month.

In many cases the first child was born nine or ten months after the ceremony, although some couples had a much longer wait. William Hiccocks, tailor, and Jodoca, his wife, waited seven years for their first born and another four years for their second child. This was an unusually long interval once the first child was born. The average interval between births was about two years, although it varied considerably. If the previous child had died at birth the interval before the next birth tended to be shorter, no doubt explained by there being no prolonged suckling of a living child to inhibit conception. It is also noticeable that, as the mother got older and the family larger, the intervals between births lengthened. This can be illustrated by the case of William Broad and his wife, Elizabeth.

Married 15 July 1621: William Broad and Elizabeth Parker
Bapt. 23 April 1622: Grace (9 months after marriage)
Buried 26 April 1622: Grace (lived 4 days)
Bapt. 16 March 1623: Elizabeth (interval 11 months)
Bapt. 13 April 1625: William (interval 2 years 1 month)
Bapt. 16 December 1627: Jane (interval 2 years 8 months)
Buried 21 December 1627: Jane (lived 1 week)
Bapt. 10 May 1629: Robert (interval 1 year 5 months)
Bapt. 20 May 1632: Nathan (interval 3 years)

Buried 1 August 1636: Nathan (lived 4 years)

Bapt. 19 February 1636: Benjamin (interval 4 years)

Buried 1 August 1636: Benjamin (lived 6 months)

It will be noticed too that the children born as their mother got older tended to be less healthy, although the fact that the last two boys were buried on the same day seems to point to them having contracted an infectious illness.

Figure 1.

The numbers of children born to 513 families living in Stratford between 1570 and 1630.*

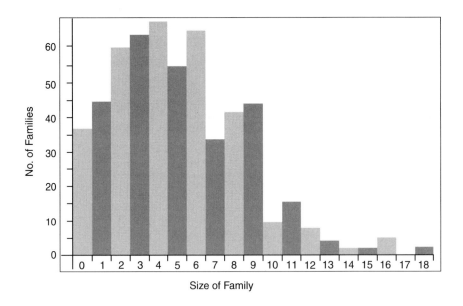

*   Between 1570 and 1599 the average number of children in the families studied was 5.56. Between 1600 and 1630 the number dropped to 5.12. J.M. Martin (1982) also noted a drop in the average number of children. His figures are: 1580–99 – 6.42, and 1600–24 – 5.61. These figures were based on all the families of the parish of Old Stratford.

While the birth of seven children in a marriage was far from unusual, it can be seen from Figure 1 that the favoured family sizes were three, four or six. It is not possible to find definite evidence of family limitation and, although it may have been practised in some cases, many of those with families of three or less lost one or more children within a week of birth which could mean difficult births and subsequent complications which precluded having further children. In several cases the early death of a partner was the reason for a small family. Few would have had the putative excuse for William Shakespeare's small family – that of the frequent absence of the father. However, like so many of their fellow townsfolk, Anne and William lost one of their three children. Young Hamnet, Judith's twin, died when he was eleven.

Among the seventy-nine larger families, of nine or more children, in fifty-one cases all were born to one mother, although Thomas Rogers's family of eighteen children was the product of two marriages. Five of his children died when less than one month old and another two at two-and-a-half months and two years. Of the average families of six children, although only one lost all of them before they reached the age of sixteen, and ten raised them all to maturity, more than half (thirty-three families of the sixty-one) lost either two or three.

If the incidence of mortality among children born within wedlock was high, that of illegitimate children was even higher. In the sixty years between 1570 and 1630, ninety-eight illegitimate babies were baptized and sixty were buried. These figures do not reflect the true situation since many of the burials are of illegitimate babies whose names do not appear among those who were baptized. Nevertheless, an entry in the burial register for 25 March 1601 which reads 'An infant found dead in Clapton Iesues' (Clopton fields) may give us a clue that, at least among the vast army of poor, 'birth-strangled babes' were not uncommon.

The number of illegitimate babies who were baptized each year rarely exceeded two, except in the years at the turn of the century when twenty-nine were baptized between 1598 and 1606, the highest number (six) being in 1599. In those cases where the father acknowledged the child, his name was entered in the register: 13 November 1595 'Margaret filia Richard Freeman, a bastard begotten on Elizabeth Smith', or, 8 January 1589 'Mary daughter of Arthur Boyes, bastard'. Arthur Boyes (usually spelt 'Boyce') was twenty-six at that time. The council arranged to pay 7s 6d towards the baby's keep until Easter when Arthur's father, Richard, agreed to take her into his home and discharge the town from keeping her.[8]

Where the father was unknown or did not acknowledge the child, and this was in the majority of cases, the entry in the baptism register might read: 21 September 1616 'Robert son of Judith Sadler, bastard', or, 7 June 1606 'Katheryn daughter to Anne Broune alias Wotton notha'. Judith Sadler, daughter of Hamnet Sadler, baker, had another illegitimate child in 1621. She was baptized Judith and was buried two days later. The father was known, or at least suspected, for Judith Sadler and William Smith of Bridgetown had been presented before the ecclesiastical court for incontinency in 1621.[9] The same was the case with Anne Broune. John Sadler had been presented before the court on a charge of incontinency with her in May 1606. She had confessed that she was pregnant and was ordered to do penance in a white sheet twice in church and once in the market place. John Sadler, aged twenty, did not appear and judgment was reserved to the next sitting, the account of which is lost, although other men in similar circumstances got away with a fine.[10] Young John, son of John Sadler the younger, yeoman, miller, gentleman, and twice bailiff, left for London soon after. There he became a successful citizen and grocer and, in 1632, presented the Corporation of Stratford with a fine mace. We do not know what happened to Anne and her daughter, Katheryn. Of the ninety-eight illegitimate baptized babies, twenty-two are known to have died within a month and eight more before they were a year old. Judith Sadler was not alone in transgressing twice. Six other cases are recorded between 1570 and 1630 and Julian(a) Wainwright had four illegitimate children within seven years, two of them dying as babies.

Since children were often named after a godparent, the same names appear in the baptism register over and over again. The 631 men in this study, together with their sons, make up almost 1,900 males and 60 per cent of these were named either John, Thomas, William or Richard. On the other hand, of the seventy-seven different names used, twenty-one appear only once. These include several from the Old Testament such as Zachariah and Obadiah and, in the case of Simon Godwin's family, twins called Ham and Japheth and his three youngest sons Sidrach, Mesach and Abednego. Among the girls there were four Rebeccas, two Abigails and a Ruth. Such names appeared in the seventeenth century when the puritan faction in Stratford was gaining ground. However, the biblical name Susannah, of which there are forty-two examples, was popular well before then. It was the name Anne and William Shakespeare gave to their first-born daughter in 1583. There were fifty-seven different names among the 1,700 women and girls, although five names made up more than 50 per cent of the total. These were Ann (which includes Anna and Agnes – frequently interchangeable), Elizabeth, Alice, Mary and Joan (or Joanna). Among the more unusual names were Timothea, Aperlyn and, rather surprisingly, Florence (spelt 'Florance' in the baptism register), a name rarely used before Mr and Mrs Nightingale chose it for their daughter. The only child who was given two baptismal names was a Clara Diana.

A child might well be given the name of a dead sibling. Nicholas Barnshurst called his eldest daughter Catherine, and five months after she died, aged eighteen months, the next Catherine was baptized. She lived to be thirteen, and three years after her death, his last daughter was christened Catherine but she lived only three months. It was more unusual to find two living children with the same name in a family, but this happened at least three times. In each case the eldest and a younger son were both called William, and they were remembered in their fathers' wills as 'son William the elder' and 'son William the younger'.

Raphe Cawdry, one of these fathers, left his son William the younger a house, when he should attain the age of twenty-one.[11] In fact, William had already reached that age when his father died six months after making the will, although his two younger sisters were aged fourteen and eleven, and a younger brother thirteen. They each received £30 under their father's will and, with their mother still alive, were well provided for. Fathers with younger children and smaller means also did their best to provide for their family. Rafe Boote, buttonmaker, left goods worth £10 and had debts owing to him of a further £9 8s. He owed £3 19s 6d, leaving close on £15, of which half went to his wife, Mary, who was his executrix and pregnant at the time, and the other half to be divided equally between his children, a son aged nine, and three daughters aged seven, five and three. Mary gave birth to another daughter, Margery, six months after her husband's death. There is no record of her remarrying and she must have found the rearing of her young family a daunting task.

When widows with small means died, leaving young children, those who had relatives or friends willing to rear them were fortunate. Otherwise the parish would take care of them. Although the phraseology of wills was often recognizably that of the scribe rather than the testator, there is no difficulty in recognizing widow Elinor Moore's own words when we read:

. . . and for that Mary my daughter is now but six years of age and being but small requireth more to breed her up to woman's estate to be able to help herself, than the small substance I have by many degrees. Therefore I give and bequeath unto her five shillings of lawful money of England to be paid unto her when she accomplisheth the full age of twenty and one years And because also I have great confidence and trust in John Mullinex the older of Old Stratford in the county of Warwick weaver, to see the breeding up of my said daughter, therefore all the rest of my goods. . . I give and bestowe on the said John Mullinex whom I ordaine and make my sole executor.

The authentic words of the testator can also be detected when Julian(a) Smith alias Court, widow of Richard, left her son, also Richard, aged twelve, £60, to be paid him when he was twenty-four, over and above the £40 left him by his father 'so that he take good ways and be ruled by the overseers'.[12] If he took evil ways he was to have £1 and the remainder of the money was to be divided between his older brothers and sisters. This fear of bad behaviour did not lessen as the children grew older. John Smyth, ironmonger, wrote a codicil to his will to the effect that if Thomas, his eldest son, then eighteen, was stubborn and would not be ruled by his mother, the house was to go to his younger brother whose lesser portion was to go to Thomas.[13] Such stipulations may well have resulted in rifts in the family and Daniel Baker was no doubt speaking from the heart when he expressed his desire that all should be settled amicably and there should be no suit of law with regard to his will. This will was complicated by the fact that, with considerable property to leave, Daniel Baker had outlived his three sons. Consequently his concern was to provide for his five grandchildren and his third wife. In most cases a family man would leave money, household goods or clothing to his children according to his means, make his wife his executrix and residuary legatee and appoint two or more male friends or relatives as overseers to assist her. The two wills which follow are typical of many. Arthur Ange was leaving a young family – his two sons were five and three. William

Greenway's family was almost grown up. Thomas Greenway at twenty-one must have been close to the end of his apprenticeship, and his sister, Katharen, was eighteen.

IN THE NAME OF GOD AMEN the xv^th day of March 1605 & in the fforthe yeare of the Rayngne of our Soverayngne Lord James by the grace of God of great bryttayne ffraunce & Ierland kyng defender of the ffayth etc. I Arthur Ange of Stratford upon Avon in the Countie of Warwyck Shoemaker beyng sycke in body but of p[er]fect memory I thanke my Lord God ordayne & make this my last will and testament in maner & forme followyng ffyrst I bequeth my Sowll unto Allmightye god trustyng to be saved by the merytts of Christes passyon & my body to be buryed in the Churchyard of Stratford aforesaid. It[em] I geve and bequeth unto my sonne Rychard Ange xl^s of lawfull money to be payd unto hym at the age of xxi^ti yeares or at the dyscretyon of myne exekatrix & Overseers It[em] I geve and bequeth unto ffrancis Ange my sonne xl^s of lawfull money to be payd unto hym at the age of xxi^ti yeares or at the discretyon of myne exekatrix & Overseers. This bequest done detts payd and legaces levyed & my body honestlye buryed then I geve and bequeth all the rest of my goods moveable and unmoveable in whose hands soever they be unto Jone my wyf who I ordayne and make my sole exekatrix of this my last wyll and testament/ And I desyre my trustye good frynds Mr Henry Wylson and Thomas hornbee to be my Sup[er]vysers of this my wyll and testament & they to have for theyr paynes therein to be taken vi^d a peece of them/

[signed] Arthur Ange. Wytnesses as followeth

I Mr Will[ia]m Gilbard als higgs scriptor
Mr Henry Wilson Robert Butler Thomas Hornby

IN THE NAME OF GOD AMEN the thirtenth day of June in
the three and fortyeth yere of the raigne of our Soveraigne Ladie
Elizabeth by the grace of god of England frannce & Ireland
Queene An[n]o dm 1601 I William Greenwaye of Stretford
uppon Avon in the Countye of Warwike beinge syck in bodie but
of p[er]fect memorie thankes be to god, do make this my last will
and testament in manner and forme following that is to say first I
bequeth my soule to almightie god my maker and redemer by
whose only merites I trust to be saved and my bodie to the earth
to be buried It[e]m I geve and bequeth to my sonne Thomas
Greenway syxe poundes xiiisiiiid to be payd unto him when the
tyme of his apprentisshippe that now he is bound to serve is come
upp: It[e]m I geve to my daughter Katharen Greenway also syxe
poundes xiiisiiiid to be paid unto her at the age of twenty and one
yeres, or at the day of mariage, yf she happen to marrie befor the
said age of xxi yeres: all the rest of my goodes moveable and
unmoveable my debtes and legacise and funerall expences
discharged I geve unto Ursula my wif whom I make my whole
and sole executrix of this my last will

witness Richard Bifield minister.

Debtes that I owe

I owe to Mr Booth of Songer	xs
It[e]m to Randle Boothe	xs
Debtes owinge me	
Roger at the bell, in Carter Lane in London oweth	
me for these	xiiiis
It[e]m Mr Nanfant oweth me	xiiiis vid
It[e]m Mr Barber oweth me	xxvs vid

William Greenway had an elder daughter, Elizabeth, aged twenty-
seven, who may well have received her portion when she married and
so was not mentioned in her father's will. This was often the case

although not invariably so. Avery Edwards left 5s to each of his four married daughters – Ursula Edkins, Margaret Ange, Ann Francis and Elizabeth Hatheway.

In both of the wills quoted, the children were treated equally. This was not always so and, although sometimes the eldest son was favoured before his brothers and sisters, this was not necessarily a matter of course either, except in those few cases where a large amount of property was involved. Often a younger son received the larger portion, although it is possible that an elder son had been set up in business some time before. This certainly happened in the case of Julius Shawe, elder son of Ralph Shawe, wooldriver. Ralph left his dwelling house to his wife Ann and, after her death or remarriage, to his younger son William who was also to receive £20 when he was twenty-one. Should he die then the house was to go to Julius and his heirs. The will then continues: to Julius 'all that stocke of money woll and other thyngs which I have already remitted into his hands to his best use and profit'. He was also to receive £17 10s to add to the £22 10s already delivered to him.

When couples were childless or the testator was unmarried the format of the will was not so predictable. Relatives and friends were made beneficiaries although relatives usually received the more substantial legacies. This was the case with Humphrey Brace, the mercer who set out in his will how his legacies and debts were to be paid. He made his wife his executrix and left her £108, two houses and the lease of a third. After her decease these were to go to his brother, Francis, and if he died without male heirs, the houses were to go to brother John to whom he left £10. He left the same sum to his two sisters and £3 each to his nephews and nieces as well as to his maid-servant. After that he listed several friends to whom he left sums ranging from 5s to £1. William Whittorne, a carpenter, with much less to leave – the goods in his inventory amounted to £20 – confined his gifts to two relatives and left everything else to his wife. His sister, Felice Danford, was to have 20s if she lived but, if she died, the money was to go to her youngest child. A further 20s were left to his sister Grace's daughter 'who came riding from Wixford to visit me'.

The 'well-beloved friends and trusty neighbours' who were appointed supervisors or overseers in most wills usually received something 'for their pains'. This could take the form of money – ranging from 6d each to £1 or more – or else a gift of clothing such as gloves or, in the case of Humphrey Brace, a dozen best silk points each. These same overseers were usually among the compilers of the inventories, at which stage they were joined by other neighbours of the deceased and, particularly when stock or tools were included in the inventory, by someone in the same line of business. Nicholas Barnshurst, woollen draper, may well have served in that capacity when the detailed stock of John Brown's shop was appraised. It was also necessary that at least one of the compilers of the inventory should be able to write and calculate although, in a substantial number of cases, the spelling is erratic in the extreme and the arithmetic poor. Relatives, friends and colleagues were also prepared to act as guarantors when a man applied for a share of one of the charitable bequests which had been set up to give young (and not so young) men a helping hand at work, or when a man or woman asked for a victualler's licence or even when bail was needed.

Acts of kindness are not difficult to find among the people of Stratford. For helping him in his sickness George Colchester left Alice Dale 5s and Frances Croft £5. John Sadler the younger agreed to pay Robert Read, the surgeon, the sum of £10 if he would attend Sadler's 'intimate friend and neighbour', John Gibbs, who had been wounded by falling timber. This act of friendship was somewhat soured by the fact that the surgeon was forced to take John Sadler to court to get the £10.[14]

Quarrels between erstwhile friends and neighbours and between husbands and wives are not difficult to find either. Nicholas Barnshurst called George Badger 'a knave and a rascal' at a council meeting and this was by no means the only time 'opprobrious words' were spoken in the council chamber. Ann, wife of John Earle the younger of Shottery, was presented by the churchwardens for calling Joan, the wife of John Rogers, a whore and bidding her go see how her bastard did.[15] Henry Field was presented for not living with his wife, Ursula. They were absent one from the other 'without order of law'.[16] The churchwardens and constables whose duty it was to present moral transgressors before the ecclesiastical court often proved themselves to be only too human when it came to transgressing. Fellow townsmen, too, were more than ready to adopt an appearance of moral rectitude and inform against their neighbours. This is a subject to which we shall turn in the next chapter.

CHAPTER FIVE

BELIEFS AND ATTITUDES

In a period when printed books were becoming both plentiful and less expensive, there were opportunities for the humble inhabitants of a small market town like Stratford to widen their horizons, *if* they had acquired the ability to read. The free school, founded by the Gild of the Holy Cross and taken over by the borough under the charter of 1553, provided a good basic education to the sons of burgesses. However, provision for a child's education does not figure widely in Stratford wills. Daniel Baker stipulated that his grandson, Samuel, was to have a larger allowance than his sisters, so that he could study at university or elsewhere, and Richard Woodward left £5 to his grandson, Richard Tyler, 'to keep him at school'.[1] Young Richard was only nine at the time and may well have been attending Stratford school, the £5 ensuring that he continued his education beyond the age of fourteen when many Stratford boys must have left to take up apprenticeships. In fact, he went on to study law and became town

'The free school . . . provided a good basic education to the sons of burgesses.'

clerk. But the presence of the school meant that, at the very least, boys in the town had the opportunity to learn to read and write. The extent of literacy is always difficult to quantify. An ability to write one's name does not necessarily point to an ability to read or, indeed, write anything other than a signature, while a fairly competent reader may not have mastered the art of writing.

Among the 800 townsfolk, there are, of course, those whose reading and writing abilities are not in doubt. Obvious examples apart from Shakespeare, are his son-in-law Dr John Hall, and John Marshall, curate of Bishopton with his large collection of books. It is taken for granted that all the clerics and lawyers were literate, and there are further examples in the neatly written notebook of Daniel Baker and the not quite so legible letters between Abraham Sturley and his 'cosen' Richard Quiney.[2] But for the majority of the townsfolk, signatures and marks are all we have on which to base our assumptions, and since it seems to be generally acknowledged that there is some correlation, however tenuous, between signatures and literacy, Table 6 may well give an indication of the position in Stratford. Well over a quarter of the 800 persons have either signed or made their mark on a document. When any clerics or lawyers who have not left signatures have been added to the former group, 163 persons could, at the very least, sign their names, and 126 made their marks.

The greatest number of examples come from the 1620s (thirty-two signatures and thirty-seven marks), but this was the only decade when the number of marks was greater than the number of signatures. In the 1590s there was evidence of thirty-one signatures and only thirteen marks.

We can see from Table 6 that, while craftsmen and craftsmen/traders were as likely to sign their names as make their marks, gentlemen, with their wider opportunities for education, those in the service category, which includes clerks and lawyers, and traders, for whom the ability to read and write was a definite asset in business, were far more

Table 6. Individuals signing or making their mark on documents between 1570 and 1630, by occupation.

Occupation	Signatures	Marks made
Craftsmen and craftsmen/traders	51	46
Traders	32	1
Agriculture	13	32
Services*	39	8
Gentlemen	8	1
Women	4	21
Unknown	16	17
Total	163	126

*See Table 3 pp. 22–3.

likely to be literate. Sixteen of the drapers and mercers shown in Table 3 could write their names and the other sixteen presented no evidence either way. Among agricultural workers the trend is reversed – almost three times as many made marks as signed and of the thirteen who could sign, twelve were yeomen.

The greatest discrepancy was, not surprisingly, among the women. Opportunities for them to witness a document were rare and there are only twenty-five examples out of the total of 289. Only one occurred before 1600. This was the mark of Margaret ap Roberts, widow, which is appended to a Corporation lease of a barn, made to her in 1598.[3] The greater number occurred after 1610 and the four signatures were all written in the 1620s. Margaret Smyth, sister to Hamnet Sadler, baker, and widow of John Smyth, vintner, signed her will in 1625 as did Elizabeth Baker, widow of Richard Baker, woollen draper, and daughter-in-law of Daniel Baker, in 1624. Margaret Kempson, daughter of John Sadler the younger, miller and gentleman, signed the bond of obligation to administer the chattels of her late husband, Leonard Kempson, gentleman, in 1625.[4] Ann Cap, who married Edward Ward, miller, in 1608, witnessed Avery Edwards's will in 1628. She is the only one who was not a wife or daughter of a member of Stratford's ruling hierarchy. Her husband was unable to write his name and made his mark when he witnessed the wills of Isabel Mecock in 1621 and John Gibbs in 1622.

While an ability to read and write was an asset for those engaged in trade, facility at computation was even more essential. Although arabic numerals were widely used at this time in other contexts, pounds, shillings and pence were written in roman numerals until well into the seventeenth century. Adding up sums of money under these circumstances is no easy task and the totals of many of the inventories are inaccurate. In most cases the discrepancy is less than £1, but twenty-eight inventories show quite large errors. The goods of Alice Williams, widow (1622), are totalled as clxiii^{l}v^s (£163 5s). In fact, the true total is £192 5s – a discrepancy of £29. Such inaccurate arithmetic could not have been confined to inventories and must have created difficulties in everyday trading.

Although a facility in both computation and writing were useful accomplishments in business, the ability to read could affect a person's life in many ways. Perhaps its greatest impact was in the sphere of religion for it enabled the ordinary man to study the Bible and also meant that he could be affected by written as well as spoken religious propaganda. Our period falls between the time of the Elizabethan Settlement and the rise of Laudian Arminianism. It was a period when the 'godly' or puritan element in the Church of England was growing in strength and when Roman Catholicism was looked on by many with fear and hatred. Both elements were present in Stratford. The puritan faction within the Corporation became more powerful at the turn of the century. It began to show its hand in the 1590s. The last payment to travelling players is entered in the chamberlains' accounts for 1593, and in December 1602 the council decreed that no plays or interludes were to be performed in the town. Anyone so licensing would be subject to a fine of 10*s*.[5] In 1611 the fine was increased to £10.[6] This hostility of the ruling oligarchy to the means by which Shakespeare earned his living must have caused a certain amount of mistrust between the council and the playwright, and surely accounted in part for his non-participation in civic affairs when he was in Stratford. The rise in power of the puritan element on the council showed itself in other ways. In the 1590s at least one alderman had Catholic sympathies. George Badger, made alderman in 1594, was frequently at loggerheads with his fellow aldermen and, after refusing to stand as bailiff in 1597, was expelled. His religion was not given as a further excuse but it would not be surprising if it played a part. By 1612, just having a recusant in the family precluded a man from serving on the council. Thomas Barbur was removed from his office as alderman because his wife was an 'obstinate recusant' and he was barred from re-election until his wife denied or altered her religion. He had been an alderman since 1571. At that time he was married to Matilda Herbach who, in 1592, was reported by the Recusancy Commission for not attending church, although it was thought age and infirmity were the causes.[7] She died shortly after and the following year Thomas married Joan Cawdry, widow of Raphe Cawdry, butcher. She too had been named by the Recusancy Commission, together with her daughter Alice, for harbouring seminaries and not attending church. One of her sons, George Cawdry, was suspected of being a seminary priest, although his whereabouts was unknown. Although there is no indication that Thomas Barbur was himself a papist, he clearly felt sympathy for them and was out of tune with many of his colleagues.

The names of some aldermen also appeared in the 1592 Recusancy Commission report for non-attendance at church. They included that of John Shakespeare, but it was thought that he and others 'absented themselves for fear of process'. The church porch was a convenient place to waylay a debtor and serve a writ. George Badger, however, was not one of those listed, though his name and those of members of his family recur in the churchwardens' presentments from 1618 onwards. He, his wife and daughter, Alice, were all presented in 1619 for non-attendance at church 'for many years' and being 'a long time excommunicate'.[8]

Recusancy was not, of course, confined to a few members of the ruling hierarchy. Within the period under discussion, fifteen persons were either accused of being recusants themselves or the charge was made against members of their families. Some were given the benefit of the doubt and their non-attendance at church put down to ill-health in old age, or poverty; others agreed to conform, but in some cases the accused clearly had the courage of their convictions. In the small hamlet of Shottery, while the wealthy Richard Woodward who owned the extensive Shottery Farm was a puritan, there were at least two families with Catholic connections. The wife of Stephen Burman was accused in the 1592 presentment of not attending church, while, in 1618, Ann, wife of Richard Burman (either Stephen's son or his nephew) was presented as a recusant papist who refused to be churched after childbirth, and in 1627 their daughter Margaret was presented as a papist. It is noticeable that it was often the womenfolk who were prepared to remain firm in their convictions. Perhaps the men were more pragmatic.

The other Shottery family with members whose attachment to the old religion is not in doubt were the Dibdales. Although John Dibdale and his wife apparently conformed, one son, Richard, was accused of being an obstinate recusant in 1592. Their eldest son, Robert, trained as a priest at Douai and, when he returned to England in 1586, was arrested, imprisoned in Newgate and hanged, drawn and quartered at Tyburn. In 1580 he had sent tokens to his family – a gilt crucifix and medal to his father, a pair of beads (a rosary) to his mother and another to his sister Agnes, and silver Roman coins to another sister.[9] This would seem to argue that, while other members of the family outwardly conformed, their sympathies lay elsewhere. This may very well have been the case with other families.

As late as the 1560s there was at least one example of a Catholic preamble to a will – commending the testator's soul to 'our blessed lady and all the holy company of heaven'. This was the will of John Jefferies the elder, a yeoman who died in 1566, who had felt it necessary to apply for a pardon when Queen Elizabeth came to the throne, for actions carried out during Queen Mary's reign. He had received the pardon for everything committed before 1 November 1558 except treason, after paying a fine of 26s 8d.[10] But in the period we are examining, any deviation from the normal protestant preamble of 'trusting to be saved by the merits of Christ's passion' is, in all probability, an indication that the testator had puritan leanings. Usually the form of words used in the preamble would be that of the writer of the will rather than that of the testator, but where there is an unusual format the testator's voice can be heard. Arthur Boyce, tailor, made his will in 1593. The preamble reads:

Firstlye I geve & bequeth my Boddye to the earthe from whence hytt came & wyllingelye yelde myselfe in thys worlde to dye sence my synnes have deserved the same & the Lorde hathe soe decreed I shulde in respecte of my synnes my sowle I commytt & comend to Christe in whose blude I assuer myselfe myne iniquityes bee purged and donne awaye & By whose alone & all suffyciente sacrifyce onnce made for my synnes & all that beleeve one hym I looke for eternall rest in the world to come, And for thes worldely thinges whereof the Lorde of his m[er]cye hath endwed me I make my disposall as followeth . . .

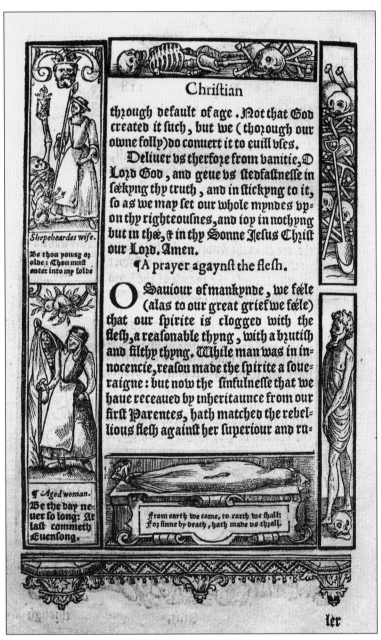

Books of prayers such as this contained many reminders of the inevitability of death for all,
from beggars to kings.

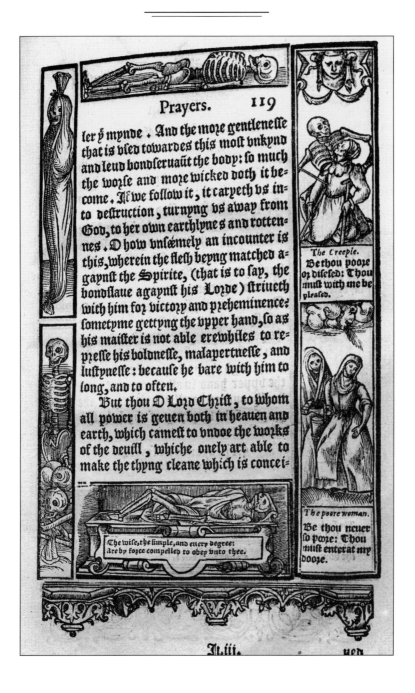

Prayers. 119

ler ẏ mynde . And the moꝛe gentlenesse that is vsed towardes this most vnkynd and lewd bondseruaūt the body: so much the woꝛse and moꝛe wicked doth it become . If we follow it, it caryeth vs into destruction, turnyng vs away from God, to her own earthlynes and rottennes . O how vnsǽmely an incounter is this, wherein the flesh beyng matched agaynst the Spirite, (that is to say, the bondslaue agaynst his Loꝛde) striueth with him foꝛ victoꝛy and preheminence: sometyme gettyng the vpper hand, so as his maister is not able erewhiles to represse his boldnesse, malapertnesse , and lustynesse : because he bare with him to long, and to often.

But thou O Loꝛd Chꝛist , to whom all power is geuen both in heauen and earth, which camest to vndoe the woꝛks of the deuill , whiche onely art able to make the thyng cleane which is concei=

The wise, the simple, and euery degree: are by foꝛce compelled to obey vnto thee.

The Creeple. Be thou pooꝛe oꝛ diseased: Thou must with me be pleased.

The pooꝛe woman. Be thou neuer so pooꝛe: Thou must enter at my dooꝛe.

Ii.iii. uen

115

Twenty-nine years later Edward Wilkes, husbandman, dictated his will which reads:

> . . . and first as concerninge my bodie even with a good will and free hart I give over comendinge yt to the earth wherof yt came nothinge doubtinge but accordinge to the article of my fayth at the great daie of gen[er]all Resureccon When wee shall appeare before the judgment seate of Christ I shall Receave the same againe, by the mightie power of god Wherew[i]th he is able to subdue all things to himself not a corruptible mortall weake and vile bodie as yt is nowe, but an uncorruptable imortall stronge & p[er]fecte body in all poynts, lyke unto the glorious bodie of my lord & saviour Christ Jesus.

There were those among the townsfolk, however, who were not prepared to follow the council's or, indeed, the Church's, lead in the matter of religion. Few went as far as Thomas Sylvester's wife who, in 1624, was presented for blasphemy – having said, 'God did doate and did he knew not what'; but John Tomlyns, tailor, before the ecclesiastical court for sabbath day misdemeanours, 'behaved irreverently' and enquired of the judge, 'Why may not I lie as well as you?'[11] Hugh Piggen's daughter-in-law reviled the vicar, Mr Wilson, calling him a knave.[12] Thomas Griffin, butcher, took out his anger on the churchwardens and constables, offering them violence and railing in the churchyard at the time of divine service.[13]

Most offenders, however, contented themselves by staying away from church and indulging in other activities, drinking, playing cards or selling goods when they should have been listening to the sermon. Humfrey Clarke, a weaver, was accused of playing his tabor and pipe in evening prayer time, and Richard Pinke's twenty-year-old son was playing at quoits at the time of divine service.[14] On the other hand, Simon Godwin, the father of Ham and Japheth, who may well have been a devout puritan, omitted to send them and his servant to be catechised. Perhaps he did not feel the established church was sufficiently 'godly'.

In 1618 the churchwardens and sidesmen, in reply to questions put at a visitation, reported that 'our Chancel is ruinous and out of repayre'.[15] The previous year the parish council had decided on a levy to be raised from parishioners towards the repair.[16] Nine parishioners from Shottery, including two members of the Burman family, together with seventeen from other parts of the parish, refused to pay. An explanation of this mass revolt may be found in the visitation report of 1618 which attributes the ruinous state to the:

> default of these men who as we suppose are bound to repair it; namely Mr William Combe for the tithes of Ryne Clifford; Mr Richard Wright [minister of Luddington] for Bridgetowne and

The Collegiate Church of the Holy Trinity, seen from the River Avon.

Clapton, Mr John Hall & Mr Henry Smith for Old Stratford & Welcombe, Mr Edward Lane for Shottery, Mr John Naish for Drayton, William Mosley for Luddington, Mr Henry Willsone for Little Wilmecote, Mr Daniell Baker for ye tithe haye of Shottery meadow.

This list includes three aldermen as well as other leading townsfolk and local gentry who rented the right to collect the tithes and were liable to contribute part of the income towards repair of the church. Edward Cottrell, who was one of the inhabitants of Shottery refusing to pay his share of the levy, was one of the sidesmen making the report. The resentment of the ordinary people against those who adopted a moral stance, yet were not themselves above blame, is understandable. Such a one was Mr John Gibbs, three times bailiff and a churchwarden who admitted to 'labouring on St. Bartholomews daye with his teame contrary to the Canons'.[17] His fine was 2d and he was dismissed. Others who committed similar offences faced stiffer fines although less able to afford them.

Those townsfolk who resented interference in their sabbath day activities may have looked on with some satisfaction when differences between leading townsmen and the vicar, Thomas Wilson, led to acrimony and suits in Star Chamber. Thomas Wilson, who had been admitted to the living in 1619, was a zealous puritan. Although at first his opponents came from among the gentry, led by John Nash and John Lane, who resented the replacement of the previous incumbent, John Rogers, by this fervent preacher, Wilson's puritan allies on the council eventually turned against him when it became apparent that he was determined to be his own man and not to be controlled by the Corporation. In these later stages of the quarrel, which continued into the 1630s, John Hall, Shakespeare's son-in-law, was Wilson's ally.[18]

The ecclesiastical court, particularly under Wilson's guidance, did not confine itself to such misdemeanours as non-attendance at church and illegal Sunday activities. It set itself up as the guardian of the people's morals and in this was greatly helped by the fact that a man's most intimate affairs were considered to be the concern of all, and few seemed averse to informing on their neighbours. Presentments to the court are full of accusations of incontinency. In view of the number of brides who were pregnant, it seems hard that, in the 1620s, some newly-weds were presented as incontinent. This happened to Ursula Sandalls who, together with her husband, Edward, was accused retrospectively, confessed and was penitent. However, there were cases, particularly among the men, where restraint was definitely called for. In 1625 Christopher Smith, a capital burgess and churchwarden, was censured for committing adultery. He refused to submit to the Peculiar (Stratford's ecclesiastical) Court and appealed to the court at Worcester. For 'weakening the liberties of the borough' and not, as might be expected, for his adultery, he was removed from the council.[19] In fact, he had been three times presented by the churchwardens, firstly for incontinency and adultery with Elizabeth Barton in July 1625, then for attempting the chastity of Joan Tarver in August 1625 and finally for incontinent behaviour towards Katharine Simmons in September 1625.[20] He had been married in 1616 and between then and 1632 became the father of seven sons and a daughter. If the accusations were true, his wife, Alice, must have been a long-suffering woman.

The Court of Record dealt with the many civil suits involving sums of money not exceeding £30, which were brought by townsfolk against their friends and neighbours. These were usually concerned with unpaid debts or such cases as that which Francis Hornby brought against Thomas Walker, accusing him of setting a dog on to bite a little pig which died.[21] Anti-social behaviour, such as having unauthorized muckheaps, selling short measure of ale or bread, or letting dogs go unmuzzled, was dealt with by the Corporation. The punishment was usually a fine which increased if the 'crime' recurred. In 1614 a whipping post was erected at the High Cross for punishing more serious offences such as begging without a licence, and by 1620 the town had a cucking stool for scolds.[22] The Corporation also dealt with matters of affray and bloodshed, provided they were not of a very serious nature.

If the number of 700 poor in the petition of 1601 (see Introduction) is correct, it is small wonder that the Corporation made sure that 'strangers' with no means of support were not welcomed in the town. As early as 1556 an order was made that no inhabitant of the borough was to harbour strange beggars, and in 1589 the wages of Richard Mekins, the beadle, were increased from 13s 4d to 20s a year, provided he did his duty in driving beggars and vagabonds out of the town. Nevertheless some townsfolk were prepared to risk censure. William Wilson was presented in 1627 for harbouring a woman delivered of a child whose husband was not known.[23] Although a poor rate was levied in response to the duty laid on the local authorities to relieve their own poor, naturally enough the local authority in Stratford was happy to allow others to take some of the burden off their hands. In February 1595, Isabel Wotton promised to discharge the town of the cost of keeping the bastard child of Edward Tomson's daughter until the child could be apprenticed.[24] Edward Tomson's daughter may well have been servant to the Widow Wotton. In fact, the child, a girl, was born in March and buried a month later. In 1609 Joan Perrot was able to enter the almshouses since her wealthy kinswoman by marriage, the widow Frances Woodward, promised to free her of keeping her granddaughter.[25]

The twenty-four almshouses never lacked occupants although a fee of 6s 8d was payable on entry. The council decided who, out of the applicants, should fill any vacancy. On more than one occasion a widow took the place of her dead husband or a widower of his dead wife, for there were no arrangements for couples to live together. This

The almshouses in Church Street

policy seems particularly harsh and inconsistent in view of the fact
that, as has been noted, when not in the almshouses, couples were
punished for not living together. In 1608 Thomas Maunton was
offered a place provided his wife and children did not come to the
almshouses to trouble the almsfolk or dwell with him. Other offers
also contained provisos such as 'so long as she behaves herself' or 'so
long as she places her child to prentice as soon as possible'. Although,
in 1586, it was decided that none should be admitted under the age
of sixty, occasional exceptions were made in the cases of blind or
crippled applicants. Several almsfolk remained there for more than
twenty years. Of the 800 people in this study, thirty-two ended their
days in the almshouses.

Money for the upkeep of the almshouses and the welfare of the inmates came from the rents of certain houses which had been donated for that purpose by gild members before the Reformation, but extra money, bread and clothing were often donated by testators in their wills. Although the doctrine of salvation through good works was no longer current, many were still prepared to give to charity on their deathbeds. The instruction to distribute bread or money to the poor or the almsfolk on the day of burial appears in many wills, often accompanied by the donation of a small sum for the repair of the church. In 1590 Thomas Wotton, weaver, asked that twenty dozen loaves should be distributed to the poor. Even at the lowest price (1*d* a loaf) this cost 20*s* out of his total goods of £15. Alice Bell, widow, also left 20*s* to the poor out of her total of £11 in 1587. The same amount was left to the poor by Richard Whiting, yeoman, in 1628, but his goods totalled £209. As the period progressed the proportion of a man's wealth which was left for charitable purposes tended to become less. The proportion of wills which included such donations also fell, from 66 per cent in the 1570s to only 31 per cent in the 1600s. There was a brief rise in the 1610s (45 per cent) and thereafter it declined again. However, in one or two cases the giving was both more generous and more specific. Daniel Baker made his will in 1637 several years before his death. He left instructions that 48*s* should be shared each year by the almsfolk, a further 26*s* 8*d* was to provide gowns for two poor widows yearly in Henley-in-Arden, and the poor of that town were to have 40*s* while the poor of Stratford were to have £4. In 1616 Ann Lloyd, widow, left £6 to be invested so that there would be 10*s* available each year to pay 6*s* to a preacher for an annual sermon and 4*s* towards repair of the church. In the same way, the 8*s* 'increase' from £4 was to be distributed annually as follows: 2*s* for the repair of the Mill Bridge, 2*s* to the chapel and 4*s* to the poor.

Others left money to be invested and lent to tradesmen or for repair of the bridge or the almshouses. But perhaps the wills which gave most pleasure to the members of the ruling hierarchy were such as that of Alice Smith, widow of Francis Smith the elder, twice bailiff, who, in 1625, left £6 to the poor of Stratford, 40s for repair of the bridge, £3 to the poor of Stow-on-the-Wold, 20s each to four men who had once been her servants to carry her body to burial – and £20 to provide a banquet for her friends.

Important events taking place on the national stage were no doubt discussed in the alehouses of Stratford and excitement must have risen considerably when townsfolk were personally involved. The fear that men chosen for the trained bands would be killed or wounded in fighting the Spanish invaders, was thankfully lifted with the news of the failure of the Armada in 1588. But at least one man from Stratford *was* maimed while fighting in Ireland on the Earl of Essex's ill-fated expedition, and the experience seems to have made him quarrelsome and, eventually, a murderer.[26] The twenty-four 'honest and sufficient' men whose names were put forward to seize the goods of Ambrose Rookwood after the Gunpowder Plot, must have felt that, for once, the small market town was involved in affairs of state.[27]

But human nature being what it is, local affairs were of most importance to Stratfordians. It did not matter that dearth and plague affected other parts of the country; it was, naturally, their own hunger and fear which exercised their minds. It was when William Combe attempted to enclose the common fields of Welcombe that Stratford became involved in petitions against the practice. In spite of the fact that customers for malt, leather goods and horses were drawn from a wide area, the overall picture which emerges is of an inward-looking community, the members of which were intensely interested in their own and their neighbours' affairs, seldom looked far for marriage partners, were slow to adopt new ideas and, for the most part, had to work hard to provide their families with the necessities of life.

With regard to the question of Stratford's fortunes between 1570 and 1630, what evidence there is does not point to a serious decline, although fire, dearth and plague did take their toll. The town shows considerable resilience after the fires of the 1590s, many of the houses being rebuilt within a few years. The chamberlains' accounts show that the Corporation's income did not suffer unduly over the next few years and in that time expenditure exceeded income by more than £3 only once. This was in 1601 when the deficit was £10 7s. In fact, income exceeded expenditure in all but twelve years out of the sixty under review, three of those years being 1570, 1571 and 1572. The last time that outgoings exceeded income was in 1623 when the deficit was £14 2s. In 1630 the council's profit was £69 17s 10d. Alan Dyer, comparing the fortunes of Stratford with other Warwickshire market towns, points out that the town had an advantage as it was the upstream terminus on the River Avon as well as the natural coaching centre between the felden (corn producing) area to the south and the forest (stock rearing) area of Arden.[28]

This book has studied the position from a different perspective, that of the prosperity of individuals calculated from their inventories, which we know often erred on the conservative side. These reveal that, whereas the average total in the 1580s was £36, it had risen to £68 in the 1620s. J.M. Martin suggests that the strict regulation of the town's social life by the council aided Stratford's economic recovery, and his calculations of individuals' wealth between 1578 and 1639 show comparable results to those arrived at in this study.[29] Inflation would account, in part, for this rise in the totals of inventories, but between 1610 and 1630 there are sufficient instances of affluence among yeomen, maltsters and innkeepers to justify the assumption that, at least in these areas, the town was flourishing. The wealth of those craftsmen/traders who worked with leather had kept pace with inflation, whereas that of other craftsmen remained static, while the wealth of labourers declined. It seems that, by the 1630s, malting, agriculture and leatherwork were helping to steady the town's fortunes. The effect on its economy of the Civil War, just over a decade ahead, is another matter.[30]

APPENDIX

The following are transcriptions of six inventories, one from each decade between 1570 and 1630.

The originals of three of the wills mentioned in this appendix are in The Shakespeare Birthplace Trust Record Office in Stratford. (Thomas Tayler: BRU 15/6/69; William Baule: BRU 15/7/148; and Elizabeth Hancocke: BRT 3/1/34). A fourth is at Hereford and Worcester County Record Office with a photocopy at Stratford (Alice Williams: PR 293/73) and that of her husband, Thomas Williams, is held at the Public Record Office in London, ref: Prob 11/133.

1. CLEMENT SWALLOW, 1571

An Invetory taken the xxiiii^th day of march in ye xiii^th of ye reiyn of Queene Elizabeth of Such goodes & cattells as Clement Swallow of Shottery in the county of Warr. gent dyed seasted off at the tyme of his dep[ar]ture beyng the xix^th of ye sayd moneyth of marche in ye yere afforesayd valued & praysed by these persons whose names & seales are under written & sette.

Imprimis one dosen of sylver spones & one odde
   spone deliveryd into ye handes of Jhon
   Myddlemore gent brother in lawe to the sayd
   Cleme[n]t praysed at   xxvi^s

Ite[m] in money there ys delyveryd into the
   handes of ye sayd John myddlemore   xli^l   xv^s

                                        or therabout

Ite[m] certayne Rynges in ye handes of ye sayd
   John myddlemore price   xxvi^s viii^d
Ite[m] viii kyne & heighfers wth iiii calves   x^l xvi^s viii^d
Ite[m] iiii yonge bestes price   iii^l
Ite[m] ii Geldynges wth saddells brydells etc iii^l   vi^s viii^d
Ite[m] wood & coale   xx^s
Ite[m] the swyne yonge & olde   xxvi^s
Ite[m] three shepe   vii^s
Ite[m] ii quarter of wheate & more   xx^s
Ite[m] in malte & barley vi quarter & vi strike or
   theraboughte price   xlvi^s viii^d
Ite[m] pease iiii strike or theraboughtes   iii^s iiii^d
Ite[m] in the parler one bedstede wth the beddynge

stooles chayers cusshyns & other furniture for a parler l^s

Ite[m] v Coffers co[n]taynynge xvii pere of shetes vii
   borde clothes iii dozen of table napkyns vi towells
   or thereabought wth other lynnen & other suche
   stuffe iii^l

Ite[m] iii other coffers & iiii caskettes price x^s

Ite[m] vi candelstyckes wth the pewter cuppes
   trenchers & other necessaryes for a buttery xxii^s

Ite[m] brasse pottes pannes cobberdes awndyrons
   trevettes spittes fyer shovells & other furnyture to
   a kytchyn

Ite[m] bakon & beyffe price xl^s

Ite[m] certayne bordes & spynnyng wheles a chese
   presse & suche like other stuffe in the bultyng house x^s

Ite[m] vessells in the bruyng house mylke house wth
   other stuff co[n]teyned in them & other houses of office xx^s

Ite[m] A malte myll wth a skele & other necessaryes in
   the myll house x^s

Ite[m] olde Iron & other stuffe in ye store house &
   other outhouses v^s

Ite[m] butter & chese xiii^s iiii^d

Ite[m] woll hempe flaxe hoppes & other necessaryes
   in the chest chamber xl^s

Ite[m] salt fyshe stock fyshe & other necessaryes in ye
   fyshe house

Ite[m] hennes geyse capons duckes wth implementes
   for those & the like houses of office x^s

Ite[m] A bell/ nettes etc. for larkyng ii^s

Ite[m] the necessary furnyture for ii servantes beddes xx^s

Ite[m] in the grete chamber a bedsted wth beddyng &
   other furnyture for a chamber xl^s

Ite[m] furniture for ii beddes in ye Inner chamber

wthin the greate chamber wth bedde posts & Ropes

etc.   xl^s

Ite[m] a flocke bedd wth other furnyture for more

servantes   x^s

Ite[m] in the Studye a presse wth hys Apparell & hyrs

there & ellswheare wth hattes cappes etc. & other

necessaryes in the same co[n]teyned   iiii^l

Ite[m] bootes spurres swyrde/dagger wth other

necessaryes for Rydynge   v^s

Ite[m] one coffer wth clothes lynynge sayes carsey &

such like stuffe   xxx^s

Ite[m] certayne lawe bookes & other bookes wth

other tryfles of small valew   vi^s

praysed by these

Robert myddleton John Dibdale X Robert Smythe X

    Suma to[tal]^{is} lxxxxvii^l ix^s iiii^d

Although it is not possible to check the accuracy of the total (£97 9s 4d) since one or two items were not valued, this is the inventory of an affluent gentleman and contains items not seen in many other inventories of a later date – such as hops, spurs and books. As the registers of Holy Trinity Church do not start until 1558 it has not been possible to ascertain when Clement Swallow married nor how many children he had. The baptism register records only two births:

  8 February 1561/2 Rosa, daughter to Clement Swallow

  17 February 1562/3 Clement son to Clement Swallow.

Since these two children were aged ten and nine when their father died, it seems likely that Clement did not live to see fifty. In neither of the entries in the register is he given the title of Mr nor referred to as 'gentleman'.

2. THOMAS TAYLER, 1587

The tru Inventory of the goodes of Thomas Tayler late of Stratford upon Avon in the county of Warwycke fuller taken the iiii^th day of october 1587 & in the xxix^th yeare of the Rayngne of our Soverayngne lady Elizabeth etc. by the discretyon of Arthur boyce Rychard Tayler & William Rogers w^t others.

In p[ri]mis his apperrell praysed at	x^s	
It[em] in the hall a table bord a forme a cheyre & a cobbord	iii^s	x^d
It[em] v pewter disshes a bason iii salts v ca[n]dlestycks at	vi^s	vi^d
It[em] a pere of Anndyrons a pere of tongs a pere of bellowes a pere of pott hooks & lynks & a fyre showll	ii^s	viii^d
It[em] a bowe viii arrowes a bill & a paynted cloth	v^s	

in the buttre

In p[ri]mis vi counterfett disshes ix sawcers iii pewter disshes fowr quart potts iii pynt potts one ca[n]dlestycke & vii stone jugges at	x^s	vi^d
It[em] iiii barrells	ii^s	
It[em] one malt myll	v^s	
It[em] iiii kevers v lomes ii sckyles a spynyng wheele ii fates iii syves p[ray]sed at	xi^s	ii^d
It[em] iii brasse potts v kettells a chaffyng disshe a dabnett ii skelletts at	xiii^s	iiii^d
It[em] a brach a pere of cobbords a frying panne a grydyro[n] a hatchett	ii^s	iii^d
It[em] a bruyng pan a boultyng tubbe	xi^s	

in the p[ar]lor & sallers

It[em] one joyned bedsted & a truclebed   x^s

It[em] v flocke bedds v coverletts one pere of
blanketts iiii pyllowes v boulsters a pere of
curtaynes at   iii^l viii^s iiii^d

It[em] one lyttle bord one forme & trestells ii
paynted clothes i other bord & forme at   ix^s iiii^d

It[em] iiii chestes iii bedsteds one presse & a bench   xv^s

in the shoppe

Inp[ri]mis ii pere of sheres one sheerebord ii
(& iii score) handlesses at   xv^s x^d

It[em] one bord & a forme & iiii smale tooles   xiii^d

Lynnens

Inp[ri]mis v pere of sheets iii bord clothes vi table
napkens thre pyllow bures one towell   xxx^s viii^d

It[em] viii stryckes of Walkers yearth   viii^s

It[em] for hey   xx^s

It[em] one mare & vii swyne   iii^l

It[em] for wodd   xxx^s

It[em] certayne planks   iiii^s

It[em] shopp teassells   ii^s vi^d

It[em] ii ladders   x^d

It[em] ii pere of pott hooks one pere of lynks &
a lanthorne   xviii^d

Som. totalis xviii^l ix^d

Thomas Tayler, a walker and fuller, who lived in Sheep Street, was
married to Sarah some time before 1575 when their first child,
Florance, was born. Her birth was followed in 1576 by that of
Margaret who lived for three weeks. Annis was born in 1577 and John
in 1579. It seems likely that John died shortly after birth, although

there is no record of his burial, since another John was born in 1581 and he lived only one week. Richard had been born in 1580 and he, too, died a week later. William was born in 1582, George in 1584 and Joan in 1586. When Thomas made his will in September 1587, he left each surviving child (two sons and three daughters aged between twelve years and nine months) £3 to be paid them at marriage or when they attained the age of twenty-one. He stipulated that, if his wife should remarry before all the children received their legacies, then bonds were to be entered into before the marriage to satisfy the children according to the will.

Sarah, who was residuary legatee and executrix, did marry again, in January 1589. Her second husband was Gilbert Charnock, a husbandman and sergeant-at-mace, who had recently buried his second wife. He had had eight children, six of whom had survived infancy, the eldest being thirty and the youngest sixteen when their father married Sarah Tayler. Sarah presented him with a son, Thomas, born six months after their marriage, and then two more daughters. Sarah died in 1606 and Gilbert married for the fourth time. This fourth wife, Margaret, died in 1615 and Gilbert died in 1618.

In Thomas Tayler's will he left his father his best coat, his brother Richard his best hat, his brother Francis his cloak and his brother William his best doublet and hose. He also left his 'book' to his brother Robert, and 2s to brother John. His two sisters, Agnes and Margaret, were to receive 5s each the following Christmas. His uncle, Arthur Boyce, and his brother, Richard, were appointed supervisors and each was to receive 2s. They also witnessed the will together with his brother Francis. The will was written by William Gilbard alias Higgs, the curate, who wrote many of the wills and inventories in the 1580s and '90s. Thomas placed a very weak mark at the end of the will.

There were lists of debts at the end of the will:

Owing to Thomas Tayler: from brother John 25s, from brother Richard 7s, from Thomas Ward for his (Thomas Tayler's) stock of cloth 3s 6d, from Richard Mayo alias Fletcher 11s, from John Lane senior for eight days work at 10d a day, 6s 8d, and from George Shacleton 12d. Total owing to Thomas: £2 14s 2d.

Thomas owed: to William Parsons £3, to Mr Richard Hill 10s, to Edward Busshell 36s and to brother Francis 6s. Total owed by Thomas £5 12s.

Other debts listed, amounting to £10 9s 6d, were crossed out and may have been repaid by Thomas in the week between the making of the will and his death. If the other debts were settled after the compiling of the inventory, Thomas's goods amounted to just under £15.

3. WILLIAM BAULE THE ELDER, 1599

An Inventorie of those goodes and Cattell whiche weare late William Baules thelders of Bishopton Deceassed Vallued and prised the 29th daye of December Anno domini 1599 by ffranncis Aynge William Aynge William Horne Thomas Cale and Thomas Greene as followeth –

Inprimis in the haule one Cobbarde one table
   boarde and a benche vallued at   iiii^s

Item one potte vallued at   iii^s

Item one cauldern vallued at   iii^s

Item two platters vallued at   xvi^d

In the Chamber Item his Apparell vallued at   v^s

Item one Coffer one Cheare vallued   ii^s   vi^d

Item one boulster one blankette one payre of sheettes
   and one boarde clothe vallued at   iiii^s

Item one Cowe vallued at   xxxiii^s   iiii^d

Item five sheppe vallued at   xvi^s   viii^d

Item two stalles of beese vallewed at   iiii^s

           The summe is iii^l xvi^s x^d

The debts owing to the said testator are   v^l   ii^s

£	s	d
8	18	10

William Baule of Bishopton made his will shortly before he died in December 1599. In it he is described as a 'labourer'. He was, apparently, a widower and, in his will, he left 10s each to his daughters, Margery and Margrete Baule, to be paid at 'Michaelmas come twelve month'. He left

10*s* each to his daughters Anne Baule and Alice Yonge (wife of Raffe Yonge) and to his son Francis. These legacies were to be paid at the feast of St Michael next, provided Francis lived that long. From this proviso we can assume that Francis was not in good health. If he did not live to receive his legacy, then the money was to go to William Baule's daughter, Elizabeth Waysacre. His youngest son, William, was to have 20*s* at 'St Michael come twelvemonth'. As well as these sums of money, Margrete was to have the cupboard in the hall, Anne a cauldron, and Elizabeth, with the consent of the eldest son, William, was to be allowed her lifetime in the chamber where the testator lay, together with all the furniture therein, also a sheep and a stall of bees. All these items are mentioned in the inventory. The bees were kept in the garden next to the hay house. Elizabeth and eldest son William were residuary legatees and executors, and neighbour William Aynge, the elder, and John Marshall, the minister, were appointed overseers and were to receive 12*d* each. From the provisions of the will we can assume that William Baule lived with his eldest son and had his own chamber which was to become the home of his widowed daughter Elizabeth.

There were debts owed to the testator which were listed at the end of the will: from Thomas Calle – 2*s*; from youngest son William – £5 to be paid as follows: 20*s* on 3 May, 40*s* on St Michael next and 40*s* on St Michael twelvemonth. It is from these sums that the legacies would be paid.

The witnesses to the will were Thomas Aynge, son of William Aynge (one of the overseers), the two William Baules, Elizabeth Waysacre and Alice Yonge (four of the testator's children), and John Marshall the minister who wrote the will.

We have here another example of two sons both called William.

4. WILLIAM SOMNER, 1606

The tru Inventory of the goodes of Willm Somner late of Stratford upon Avon in the Countye of Warwycke Carpenter taken the xxith day of August in the iiiith yeare of the Rayngne of our Soveryngne lord James by the grace of God kyng of Ayngland, ffrannce & Ierland defender of the ffayth by the discretyon of Mr Henry Wilson & John Smith.

Inp[rimis] in the hall a tablebord w^t a frame a
   cobbord a bench a form ii kyvers, ii stowells a
   lyttle barrell   xiii^s iiii^d

It[em] ii platters ii pewter dishes, ix sawcers one
   salt ii smale Candlestyckes on brasse pott
   ii kettles at   x^s

It[em] one pere of bellows, pott hookes, pott lynks,
   a grydyron, a bra[n]dard, a frying panne ii smale
   shilves a brache & a lyttle forme, disshes, trenchers
   spones & other smale Impleme[n]ts   iii^s iiii^d

                    in the Chamber

It[em] all his workyng tooles at   x^s

It[em] all his weryng apperrell   x^s

It[em] ii bedsteds   ii^s

It[em] an old flocke bed a blankett an old throme
   cloth, a red saye, an old hillyng, thre boulsters
   one pillowe at   ii^s iiii^d

It[em] iii pere of sheetes a bord cloth ii table
   napkyns a pillow bure, ii hand wypers   vii^s

It[em] thre coffers a boultyng which & one other

barrel ii lyttle formes wyth other Implements of wod   vii^s

It[em] wod & chypps   v^s

[In a different hand]

It[e]m iii quart[ers] and vii strike of malt   iii^l

Some is iiii^l xii^d

[The last £3 is not included in the total]

William Somner, a carpenter, married Isabella Salter in 1590. Their first son, Richard, was born ten months later and only lived eight days. A year later a daughter, Frances, was born. They buried an unnamed infant in 1595 and then had another daughter, Katherine, in 1596 and a son, Thomas, in 1599. Isabella died in 1604 and William married again five months later. His second wife, Anne Wyllyams, bore him a son, William, in 1605, and a year later William Somner senior died.

Soon after her father died, Katherine, then aged ten, was apprenticed to Jane Lummas, a seamster, for seven years. There is no record of what happened to young Thomas, aged seven. Perhaps he continued to live with his stepmother and little stepbrother. Frances, aged fourteen when her father died, was probably already apprenticed.

5. ELIZABETH HANCOCKE, 1619

The Inventory of Elizabeth hancockes goodes late of Stratford upon Avon in the Countie of Warr. Spinster deceased valewed and praised the xxviii[th] of January 1619 by Robert Williamson gent Thomas Lea John Eame George Bray Richard Rennoldes Robert Ingram and Henrie P[ar]son.

Inprimis one pott and one Calderne	xiii[s]	iiii[d]
Item iiii platters one chafing dish one salt seller and one sawcer	vi[s]	viii[d]
Item one peire of sheetes and one little peece of cloth	iii[s]	vi[d]
Item three smockes and three old partlettes	iiii[s]	iiii[d]
Item one peire of bodies one Carcheife and one table napkin	iii[s]	vi[d]
Item one purce one apron one peire of little silver hooks one pin of silver and one girdle	iiii[s]	vi[d]
Item twoe old little baggs		xii[d]
Item one little box		xii[d]
Item one stuffe gowne and one meddly gowne	xiii[s]	iiii[d]
Item one petticote and one apron	x[s]	
Item one hatt	iii[s]	iiii[d]
Item one old gowne one safegard	iii[s]	iiii[d]
Item one keverlet and one old peece of green cloth	ii[s]	viii[d]
Item twoe blanckettes a peece of cloth and one old wastcote	vi[s]	
Item twoe old petticotes		xii[d]
Item twoe kettles one Candlesticke and one frying pan	v[s]	iiii[d]
Item one brush one peire of sheires and one old apron		vi[d]

Item one feather bed one flocke pillowe one quishion
    and one flag mat   —   x^s viii^d

Item Twoe coffers and one hamp[er]   ii^s vi^d

Item one strike   xii^d

Item one Spitt and other ymplem[en]ts   xii^d

Item one bedstead one board one little wheel   ii^s

Item foure quarters and ii strikes of malt in the
    handes of George Badger   iii^l viii^s

Item five quarters of malt in the hands of William
    Wyett gent   iiii^l

                  Soma Totalis xii^{l}viii ^{s} ii^d

sg.   R. W[illia]^{m}son

        Thomas Lea

        Henry P[ar]sone

Elizabeth Hancocke, a spinster, did not leave a written will but, according to witnesses, Elizabeth Ison, her son Henry Ison and Thomas Lea, she called to her nephew, Thomas Bendford, saying:

> Coozen I doe intend to live & end my dais with you And to that end I doe absolutely give unto you Coozen All my goodes I have moveable & unmoveable except ffoure mill sixpences I have which I give to fowre poore men to carry my bodie to buriall and do make you my Executor.

She gave him £8. This nuncupative will was proved in February 1619.

6. ALICE WILLIAMS, 1622

A true and p[er]fect Inventarie of the goods and Cattles of Alice
Williams late of Stratford uppon Avon in the Countie of Warwicke
widdowe deceased/ taken and praysed the first day of November 1622
by Anthony Smithe Richard Robbins Henrie Norman and Thomas
ffisher.

In primis in Readie monye ringes jewells and plate	xl*l*	x*s*	
Ite[m] her wearinge apparell	xv*l*		
Ite[m] in the hall: i long table, i little table six ioyned stooles, i chayre, fyve lowe stooles one forme, i chest, i waynscott cubbord, i baken Rack, one payre of playing tables, one cupbord stoole & fower little bordes	i*l*	xii*s*	
Ite[m] i peece of waynscott and a waynscott portall		vi*s*	
Ite[m] one Iron Jack		xiii*s*	
Ite[m] i dripping pan, i paire of andirons, i grate bellowes, lynkes, potthookes, fyer shovell tongs and other Iron ware there		xvii*s*	
Ite[m] 2 great brasse pans, 3 kettles i warming pan & 2 skim[m]ers	iii*l*	ii*s*	vi*d*
Ite[m] 4 small brasse pottes, 3 posnettes, i spice morter & pestle & a brasse spoone		xvii*s*	vi*d*
Ite[m] in baken		iii*s*	
Ite[m] in the buttrye: i saue, i chest, i little table i powdring tubbe, salt, barrells, i skuttle, bottles, trenchers, shelves and other trump[er]ie	i*l*	iiii*s*	
Ite[m] in the Shoppe: cowp[er]ie ware shelves and other trump[er]ie		x*s*	

Ite[m] in the Millhouse: i maltmill, coles, a garden
    Rake, 2 shepikes, i spade and other trump[er]ie   xviii*s*   vi*d*

Ite[m] in the yard: in wood, coles, tressils, i ladder
    i washtocke & peasestraw   xiii*s*   iiii*d*

Ite[m] a lanthorne   vi*d*

Ite[m] in the little chamber: all her pewter i brasse
    chafingdish one brasse candlestick and a paire of
    brasse scales   ii*l*   xi*s*   vi*d*

Ite[m] i table, 2 chaires, six boxes, 3 trunckes i chest,
    i syde saddle and clothe w*th* bridle & furniture,
    one pillian w*th* an old clothe to it   i*l*   xvi*s*

Ite[m] one lookinge glasse   iii*s*

Ite[m] bookes there   xiii*s*   iiii*d*

Ite[m] i cheese cratch, 2 meale sives and other
    trump[er]ie   iii*s*

Ite[m] in the chamber over the hall: 2 standing
    bedsteedes & a truckle bedsteed   *l*   x*s*

Ite[m] 2 featherbedes & 4 bolsters, i flockbed,
    2 strawbedes, 2 sett of curtaines & rodes &
    3 pillowes   v*l*

Ite[m] 3 payre of blankettes i greene Rugge &
    2 other coverleades   ii*l*

Ite[m] sheetes, pillowbeares, table clothes napkins
    & other small lynnens   v*l*   iiii*s*

Ite[m] eight cusshions   xiii*s*   vi*d*

Ite[m] i great chest and 2 trunckes   xx*s*

Ite[m] in Mault   v*l*

Ite[m] all other small ymplementes and trump[er]ie
    of all sortes   iii*s*   iiii*d*

Ite[m] owinge to the testatrix in debts, uppon
    specialties   C*l*

Some totalis Clxiii*l* v*s*

Anthonye Smith [signature]

Tho: ffisher [signature]

Henry Narmons
his marke

Richard Robbins [signature]

Alice Williams, widow of Thomas Williams, gentleman, who had died in 1613, was clearly a wealthy woman by Stratford standards. As well as the items set out in her inventory, her husband had left her all his 'messuages, lands, tenements, hereditaments, revercions, profittes and commodities wheresoever situate in the counties of Gloucestershire and Warwickshire'. She also received all his goods, chattels, plate and jewels – his apparel only excepted – and these do appear in the inventory. His brother, James, was to have his apparel. Alice was made his executrix and he referred to her as his 'well beloved wife'.

When Alice came to make her will in 1622 she expressed a wish to be buried near her husband. They do not appear to have had any children. She left various bequests to people outside Stratford – one living as far afield as Petworth in Sussex. But the people of Stratford were not forgotten. Mr Wilson, the vicar, was left 20*s* to give a sermon, and twenty nobles to provide a dinner after her funeral. (A noble was worth 6*s* 8*d*.) The poor of Stratford were to receive £3 6*s* 8*d*, and twenty nobles were to set two poor tradesmen or young beginners up in work, and the increase from this was also to go to the poor. Alice left the sum of £13 6*s* 8*d* to a certain Alice Nicholls, 20*s* to Jillian Allen and 10*s* to Goodwife (Jone) Hammons, a neighbour. Alice, the wife of Robert Butler, was to have her best gown, petticoat and apron. All these women were from Stratford and the two Alices may well have been goddaughters of the testatrix. The joint executors and residuary legatees were Mr Francis

Ange, Mr William Walford and Mr Robert Butler – all members of Stratford's ruling hierarchy. The overseers were William Greene of Beoley and William Higgins of Stratford. Three of the four witnesses were women: Joan Hammons, Margaret Higgins and Elizabeth Ange. The fourth was Thomas Fisher, one of the compilers of the inventory.

GLOSSARY

anfyle	anvil
anndiornes	andirons – metal supports to hold wood in
(awndyrons, anndyrons)	the fireplace, sometimes called fire dogs
aparne (aporn)	apron
apre ware	napery
balles	bellows
bands	neckbands
baize	in the sixteenth century, a fine light material
bastard loom	an inferior type of loom
bay	(a) a large alcove in a barn, or (b) a division of a house. A house of three bays would have three large windows along the front
beaker	a type of cup without a handle
bill	a billhook – a tool with a curved or hooked blade used for pruning, etc.
blese	a blaze – a white mark on a horse's forehead
bodies (pair of)	a bodice
bonlase	bone lace – made with bone pegs
boulting (bolding, bulting)	sieving – a 'boulting wich' is a sieving bin
braches	spits
brandard	a brandiron or grid
broadcloth	fine wide plain cloth
brokes	instruments for dressing hemp or flax
buckler	a small shield

145

burgage	a plot of land, in Stratford measuring 3½ perches by 12 perches (52 ft x 198 ft) for which a rent of 12*d* a year was paid to the lord of the manor
buttery	a service room where ale (and sometimes food or general stores) were kept
buttris	a hoof-paring tool
bychorne	a two-pronged instrument used by smiths
calderne	cauldron
calliver	a type of light musket
canvas	fine unbleached cloth
carchowes (carcheifes)	kerchiefs – cloths used to cover the head
carsey	see *kersey*
chaffinge dish (chafing, chaffyng)	a dish to set on a chaffer (a small enclosed brasier containing hot coals for heating food and drink)
chamlett	material, originally fine and from the east, but later the name given to any fine wool, silk, haircloth, cotton or linen
cheese cratch	a rack for storing cheeses
cherurgerie	chirurgery – surgery
Chess	Cheshire
chesselle	a chisel
citterne	a sort of guitar with wire strings, played with a plectrum
close stool	a commode
cobbarde (cobbord)	a cupboard
cobberds (pair of)	cobirons – often employed instead of andirons – long bars fitted with hooks at frequent intervals. Two cobirons leant against the back of the fireplace at an angle of 45° and the ends of the spit were

	placed at whichever pair of hooks was most suitable
coffer	a small chest or strongbox to keep valuables in
corviser	a shoemaker – originally one who worked in Cordoban (fine) leather
counterfett	The exact meaning in the Stratford inventories is obscure. Suggestions are that it was: (a) an inferior type of dish in a material resembling pewter, (b) a type of porringer, or (c) an object that was made from a pattern
cotherne	cauldron
cotton	in the sixteenth century, a cheap woollen material
couch house	an outhouse where barley was spread to dry
cowperyware	wooden barrels, etc. – made by a cooper
coverleades	coverlets
crescloth	a crosscloth – a knitted kerchief
crusses	cruises – drinking cups
culbe	a retort or bowl
dabnettes	dabnets – small cooking utensils
doge	this could mean 'dog' (andiron), but in Ballamy's inventory it is more likely to be a smith's tool
dornix	a coarse sort of damask used for carpets and curtains, first manufactured in Tournai (Dornick in Flemish)
doublet	a man's short, close-fitting jacket
doung fork	a dung fork
dow skin	doe skin

downey	down (feathers)
dresser	a side table for dressing meat, etc.
draughtnet	a fishing net
ewting fatt	see *uting fate*
fates	vats
fetches	vetches – for fuel
fiddle cloth	probably a cloth used as a violin rest under the chin
flag mat	a rush mat
flaxen	fine linen material – woven from flax
flock	wool refuse used for stuffing mattresses, cushions, etc.
forehammer	the large hammer which strikes first
frieze	a coarse woollen cloth with nap on one side
fuller	a clothworker using fuller's (or walker's) earth, an absorbent clay which removes grease from cloth in the fulling process. A fuller could also be referred to as 'a walker' and fulling was often done by shearmen
fyre showle	a fire shovel
gounde	a gown
greires	gears – harness or chains, wheels, etc.
grenddlestone	a grindstone
gridyrne (grydyron)	a gridiron – a grid or iron bars on feet, with a long handle, used for cooking over a fire
grogram	coarse fabric of silk or mohair, often stiffened with gum
hachet	a hatchet
hancarchond	a handkerchief
handlesses (hanglesses)	the exact meaning is unclear, but they

	were used in large quantities by shearmen and therefore *handless* was probably the local word for a tenterhook. Tenterhooks attached the cloth to the stretcher or tenter
haninges	pieces of iron or chains fixed to the chimney on which to hang pothooks
hates (hattes)	hats
hatt bonds	hatbands
hempen	coarse fabric made from hemp (the cannabis plant)
herecloth	coarse open fabric made from horse hair and used to hold the malt drying over the kiln
hewing blades	axes
heyfer (heighfer)	a heifer – a young cow which has not had a calf
hilling	a bed covering
hogshead	a large cask holding 52½ imperial gallons
horse lock	a shackle to keep the horse still while it was being shod
hurden	coarse material woven from flax
hurst stafe	a wooden staff
jack	a handle
jerkin	a close-fitting jacket, often made of leather
kench	a weight of wheat, the amount varying according to place
kersey	coarse, narrow cloth woven from long wool, usually ribbed
kertle	kirtle – a woman's garment – an outer petticoat

kettle	an open cooking pot with handles on both sides
keverlet	a coverlet
kine	cows
kyver (kever)	a shallow wooden tub
lande	a strip of arable land in the open field, about half an acre
Lanke	Lancashire
lattice cupboard	a cupboard with an open-work door
lead	a cauldron
lincks (lynks)	(a) chains, or (b) torches made of tow and pitch carried in the street at night
lome	an open vessel or tub
maling cords	ropes for tying packs onto horses
mark	a coin worth 13s 4d
mattoke	an agricultural tool for loosening hard ground
meddly	material of mixed colour or type
napkins	table napkins – essential items since food was eaten with the fingers
nawger	an auger – a carpenter's tool for boring holes in wood
necloth	neckerchief
neeld	needlework
orrise	a type of lace
packcloth	cloth to place under the pack saddle or to wrap goods in for carriage
pack saddle	one on which packs were carried
painted cloths	cloth or canvas painted with patterns of flowers or mottoes or with religious scenes. A cheap substitute for tapestry
partlet	linen to cover the neck and shoulders

pidg	a pig
pillowbear (pillowbure)	a pillow case
plater	a platter – a flat dish or plate of pewter or wood
playing tables	tables for playing cards on. They were also marked out for a board game – backgammon or chess
plecke	a small enclosure
points	tagged laces or cords for tying hose to a doublet or for lacing a bodice
porringer	a porridge bowl, often with a lid and handle
portal (portall)	a wooden framed screen attached to the inside of the door to keep out draughts
posnit (posnet, posnette)	a small metal cooking pot with three feet and a handle
powdering tub	a tub in which meat was cured with salt or spice
prechel	an instrument for punching holes in horseshoes
presse	a large cupboard with doors and shelves for storing clothes, linen, etc.
putcheon	an eel trap
pynner	(a) a pinafore, or (b) a coif with two long strips on either side for fastening – worn by women of quality
pynsonnes	pliers
quarter	a measure of capacity of grain. Traditionally 8 bushels
quife	a coif – a close fitting cap covering the head – worn by both sexes
quishion	cushion

recorder	a wooden instrument – the forerunner of the clarinet
reveting	riveting
ruffes	exaggerated collars
safegard (savegard)	an outer skirt to protect the main skirt when riding
sallet dish	a dish for salad
saue	a saw
sawcer	a dish for sauce
saye	fine silk or serge
sconce	(a) a lantern or candlestick with a screen to protect it from the wind, or (b) a bracket candlestick fixed to the wall
seamster	a seamstress – one who does fine sewing for a living
sheerebord	a table on which cloth is sheared
sheires	shears
shepyke	a pitchfork
shilves	shelves
shule (showll)	a shovel
shws	shoes or horseshoes
skeles (sckyles)	(a) scales for weighing, or (b) drinking cups
skene	a dagger
skillet (skellet)	a cooking vessel. A larger version of a posnet
skimmer (skymer)	(a) an iron instrument for taking ashes from the hearth, or (b) a cooking ladle
skipp	a basket or a container
smocke	a shift or under-petticoat
solar	an upper room, often with a large window to catch the sunlight
specialty	a special contract or bond made under seal

spence	a service room – usually a storeroom or larder
spitte	a slender, pointed rod of metal or wood used for thrusting through meat which then revolved and roasted before the fire
stafe pyck	a pitchfork
standing bed	one standing out into the room with corner posts, curtains, tester and vallances
steers	young castrated oxen
stockfish	fish which has been dried without the use of salt
stock lock	a lock enclosed in a wooden case, usually fitted to an outer door
stoke	a stock – a support
stole (stowell)	a stool
stomacher	an ornamental covering for the chest, worn under the lattice of a bodice
store pig	a nearly fully grown pig
stryke (strike)	one eighth of a quarter – a bushel. In some areas it was half a bushel.
taffatie	taffaty – in the sixteenth century, a fine silken or linen cloth
tavern	an outhouse or cellar
teassells	teasels – bristly plants, the seed heads of which were used to raise the nap on cloth
tenements	dwelling places
tester	a canopy over a bed, supported by posts or hanging from the ceiling. It could also mean a headboard
thrum (throme)	fringed cloth
tiffanie	thin transparent gauze or fine gauze muslin

tod	a bundle of wool weighing 28 lb
treen	wooden ware – plates, etc.
trencher	a large flat plate of wood
trevett	a trivet – a three-footed metal stand for a pot or kettle, put in front of or over the fire
truclebed	a truckle bed – a low bed on castors which could be rolled under a higher bed when not in use.
trye	a sieve or a screen for sifting
tumbrel	a two-wheeled cart
turkey	material woven on a loom in imitation of a Turkish carpet
twilly	a coarse linen fabric covering for a bed
uting fate	a vat where the barley was soaked prior to making malt
verinshe (verinice)	a superior type of tobacco named after a town in Venezuela, its place of origin
viall	a viol – a stringed instrument played with a bow
virginalls (pair of)	a keyed instrument, similar to a spinet without legs, played on a table
wainscot	panelling
wall-bed	one fixed to the wall, sometimes with doors
wampty	a surcingle – a strap to go under a horse's belly
warping bars	part of a weaver's loom
washtocke	wash stock – probably a wooden club for beating clothes when they were being laundered
whittawer	a glover – one who works with white leather

whoppe	a hoop – a quart measure
wiche (which)	a bin into which flour or meal is sifted
wooldriver	a man who bought wool from the producer to sell to the clothmaker
wrought	embroidered
wymble	a gimlet
yeeling house	a brewing house
yerene	iron.

NOTES

Abbreviations used in the Notes

Cal. WW (1)   *Calendar of Wills and Administrations in the Consistory*
               Court of the Bishop of Worcester 1451–1600, ed. E.A. Fry,
               British Record Society Ltd, 1904.

Cal. WW (2)   *Calendar of Wills and Administrations in the Consistory*
               Court of the Bishop of Worcester 1601–1652, ed. E.A. Fry,
               British Record Society Ltd, 1910.

CBB   Council Book B. SRO BRU 2/2.

CBC   Council Book C. SRO BRU 2/3.

M&A   *The Minutes and Accounts of the Corporation of Stratford-*
               upon-Avon and Other Records 1553–1598, vols 1–4
               transcribed by Richard Savage, introduction and notes
               by Edgar J. Fripp. Vol. 5 edited by Levi Fox. Dugdale
               Society.
               Vol. 1. 1553–1566 (1921)
               Vol. 2. 1566–1577 (1924)
               Vol. 3. 1577–1586 (1926)
               Vol. 4. 1586–1592 (1929)
               Vol. 5. 1592–1598 (1990)

PRO   Public Record Office, London.

SRO   Shakespeare Birthplace Trust Record Office, Stratford-
               upon-Avon.

STC   *A Short-title Catalogue of Books printed in England,*
               Scotland and Ireland 1475–1640, first compiled by
               A.W. Pollard and G.R. Redgrave, 2nd edn, London,
               Bibliographical Society, 1986, 3 vols.

VCH   *The Victoria County History of the County of Warwick:*

Vol. 3, Barlichway Hundred, general editor L.F. Salzmann, local editor Philip Styles, 1945.

War. RO   Warwickshire County Record Office, Warwick.

Introduction

1. SRO BRU 15/5/157.
2. J.E. Jones, 'A Community Study of Sixteenth-century Stratford-upon-Avon' (unpublished M.Phil. thesis, University of Birmingham, 1991), pp. 14, 15 and Appendix 2.
3. Alan Dyer, 'Warwickshire Towns under the Tudors and Stuarts', *Warwickshire History*, Vol. III, No. 4 (1976/7), p. 133.
4. SRO BRU 15/5/7.
5. P. Clark and P. Slack, *English Towns in Transition* (Oxford University Press, 1976), pp. 97–103. Their suggestion is that such temporary misfortunes were overcome in some towns.

Chapter One

1. SRO BRU 15/7/79, BRU 8/15/12, PRO Will of Richard Hill, 1593, Prob 11/83.
2. SRO Corporation leases BRU 8/10.
3. SRO Corporation leases BRU 8/6.
4. SRO BRU 4/1 Chamberlains' Accounts, 1604.
5. War. RO Greville Papers CR 1886 Z 133. Inquisition Post Mortem of Ambrose Dudley, Earl of Warwick, 1590. The part of the Inquisition which applies to Stratford is transcribed and published in *M&A*, vol. 4, pp. 92 ff.
6. SRO BRU 15/12/95 1608.
7. *M&A*, Vol. 3, pp. 26, 133, 148. CBB 29 January 1603/4.
8. *Cal. WW* (1) Will of John Sadler, No. 21, p. 288, 1584.
9. Although surnames or family names were generally settled before this period, some families were still known by two surnames, one perhaps being drawn from the occupation of an ancestor or the female line, and the other from the male line.
10. SRO BRU 15/3/41.
11. SRO BRU 9/1/2.
12. SRO ER 2/28.
13. SRO ER 2/24.

14. SRO ER 27/11.
15. SRO ER 2/19. A mark was worth 13*s* 4*d*.
16. *M&A*, Vol. 2, pp. 79–85. Corporation survey 10 March 1573/4, SRO ER 1/1 f.40, War. RO Greville Papers CR 1886 Z 133.
17. Kent County Record Office, Maidstone. U 269/E 249/6.
18. SRO BRU 8/1–8/15.
19. CBB 9 December 1608.
20. *Cal. WW* (1) Will of Richard Ballamy, No. 62, p. 271, 1581.
21. *M&A*, Vol. 3, p. 106.
22. War. RO Greville Papers CR 1886 BB 711/2663. Partly printed in *M&A*, Vol. 5, pp. 48–70.
23. The totals of all inventories will be given to the nearest pound to avoid confusion.

Chapter Two

1. *M&A*, Vol. 4, p. 115.
2. It must be remembered that these were the occupations of people who lived between 1570 and 1630 and, therefore, were not all following their occupation at the same time. Among the twenty-four tailors, ten were active between 1580 and 1590, although the average number in any decade was seven. It is, however, likely that there were other tailors working in the town who are not included among the persons in this study. Visitors to the weekly market would have given orders for new garments and alterations to old ones since the needs of the inhabitants of Stratford alone would not have provided sufficient work to keep so many tailors employed. The glovers, on the other hand, would have made gloves for sale and would not rely on specific orders. In the decade from 1610 to 1619, thirteen of the twenty-three glovers were plying their trade although the average number working in each decade was eight.
3. PRO Will of John Wall, 1615, Prob 11/126.
4. *Cal. WW* (1) Will of Thomas Wotton, No. 89, 1591.
5. SRO BRU 17/1.
6. SRO BRU 15/12/67.
7. SRO BRU 15/12/63.
8. SRO BRU 15/9/22 and 15/12/50.
9. SRO BRU 15/1/115.
10. SRO BRU 12/1.

11. *M&A*, Vol. 5, pp. 132 & 133, 1598.

12. *VCH*, Vol. 3, p. 236.

13. War. RO Greville Papers CR 1886 BB 708/1638.

14. P. Laslett, *The World We Have Lost – Further Explored*, 3rd edn (Cambridge University Press, 1983), p. 29.

15. SRO BRU 15/7/30.

16. SRO BRU 15/14/1, BRU 15/14/2.

17. PRO Will of Roger Sadler, 1578, Prob 11/61.

18. SRO BRU 4/1 Chamberlains' Accounts, 1615.

19. SRO BRU 4/1 Chamberlains' Accounts.

20. It is virtually impossible to convert amounts of money into their modern equivalents. Today's consumer economy, manufacturing methods and higher standard of living in Britain preclude comparison of like with like. Decimalization and inflation also have to be taken into account. If we look at wages, a minimum wage of £3.50 an hour is considered necessary by most people at the present time. An eight-hour day would yield £28 or 560 shillings in pre-decimal coinage (12*d* = 1*s*, 20*s* = £1, 240*d* = £1). An unskilled worker in the sixteenth century would do well to earn 10*d* a day. This means a multiplying factor of over 650 would be necessary to convert sixteenth-century wages to those of the twentieth century.

21. SRO BRU 15/1/106, ER1/115/56, ER1/115/59.

22. CBC 26 January 1630/1.

23. CBB and CBC.

24. J.O. Halliwell, ed., *An Inventory of the Furniture etc. of a Tavern in Stratford-upon-Avon taken in the time of Shakespeare*. The book is undated but its contents were reprinted from *Collectanea Archaeologica: Communications made to the British Archaeological Association*, Vol. 2, 1862–4.

25. PRO Will of Thomas Williams, 1619, Prob 11/133.

26. SRO BRU 4/1 Chamberlains' Accounts, 1604.

27. SRO ER 82/6/93 Item 37. This is a handwritten transcription of Robert Johnson's inventory. The original document, formerly held in Worcester, is not now listed in *Cal. WW* (2).

28. *Cal. WW* (1) Will of John Robins, No. 120, 1588.

29. SRO BRU 12/7 and BRU 12/8.

30. PRO Will of Humphrey Brace, 1591, Prob 11/79.

Chapter Three

1. *Cal. WW* (1) Will of William Smarte, baker, 1593, p. 357, No. 93.
2. *Cal. WW* (1) Will of John Sadler, 1584, p. 288, No. 21.
3. PRO Will of Thomas Williams 1619, Prob 11/133.
4. This was probably *The Works of Richard Greenham*, edited by Holland, the third edition of which appeared in 1601. Greenham was the rector, from 1571 to 1591, of Dry Drayton, the first model Puritan parish in England.
5. PRO Nuncupative will of John Hall, 1635, Prob 11/172.
6. SRO ER1/61 f44 Saunders Collection. This is a transcript of Marshall's inventory but with no indication of the whereabouts of the original.
7. *An Apologye of Syr Thomas More*, published 1533.
8. *Enchiridion Militis Christiani*, a manual of piety written in 1503 and translated into English by William Tyndale, and *Colloquia*, described as vivid and entertaining in *The Oxford Companion to English Literature*, 4th edn (Oxford University Press, 1975), p. 275.
9. STC. 19429.5. J. Partridge, *The Treasure of Hidden Secrets. Commonlie called the good huswives closet* (newly enlarged, R. Johnes, 1596).
   STC. 793.7. *The Arte of Angling* (H. Middleton, 1577). A dialogue betweene Viator and Piscator. Has been attributed to W. Samuel and Dr W. Ward.
   STC. 4700. Jean de Cartigny, *The Voyage of the wandering Knight*. Devised by J. Carthenie and translated out of French by W. Goodyear [ed.] (R. Norman) T. East, 1581.
10. STC. 1086. Gervase Babington, *Certain plaine, brief and comfortable notes upon everie Chapter of Genesis* (A. Jeffes, P. Short) f. T. Chade, 1596.
11. PRO Will of Alice Smyth, widow 1584, Prob 11/68.
12. F.J. Furnivall (ed.), *Harrison's Description of England in Shakspere's Youth: The Second and Third Books*. Part 1, *The Second Book* (New Shakspere Society, Series VI, 1877), pp. 236, 240.

Chapter Four

1. War. RO Greville Papers BB 711/2663.
2. *Cal. WW* (2) Will of Thomas Hiccocks, yeoman, 1611, p. 46, No. 61.
3. SRO BRU 8/9/5.
4. SRO Council Book B. 19.7.1598.
5. SRO BRU 15/13/106.
6. Laslett, *The World We Have Lost*, p. 82.

7. J.M. Martin, 'A Warwickshire Market Town in Adversity', *Midland History*, Vol. VII (1982), pp. 28–38.

8. *M&A*, Vol. 4, p. 77.

9. SRO BRT 4/1/1.

10. E.R.C. Brinkworth, *Shakespeare and the Bawdy Court of Stratford* (Chichester, 1972), p. 131.

11. PRO Will of Raphe Cawdry, 1588, Prob 11/73.

12. PRO Will of Juliana Smith alias Court, 1593, Prob 11/81.

13. PRO Will of John Smyth, ironmonger, 1613, Prob 11/121.

14. SRO BRU 15/6/176.

15. SRO ER 1/115/51.

16. SRO ER 1/115/f4.

Chapter Five

1. PRO Will of Richard Woodward, gent., 1601/2, Prob 11/99.

2. SRO ER 1/76, BRU 15/1/134–46, DR 328/14/1.

3. SRO BRU 8/3/4.

4. SRO BRU 15/13/76.

5. CBB 17 December 1602.

6. CBB 7 February 1611.

7. War. RO Greville Papers CR 1886 BB 711/2662.

8. SRO ER 1/115/13.

9. PRO SP 12/179/4.

10. *M&A*, Vol. 1, p. 45.

11. SRO ER 1/115/48, and Brinkworth, *Shakespeare and the Bawdy Court*, p. 53.

12. SRO ER 1/115.

13. SRO ER 1/115.

14. SRO ER 1/115, and Brinkworth, *Shakespeare and the Bawdy Court*, p. 129.

15. SRO ER 1/115.

16. SRO ER 1/115.

17. Brinkworth, *Shakespeare and the Bawdy Court*, p. 144.

18. Ann Hughes, 'Religion and Society in Stratford-upon-Avon 1619–1638', *Midland History*, Vol. XIX (1994), pp. 58–78.

19. CBB 7 September 1625, and SRO BRU 15/13/70.

20. SRO ER 1/115/53, 55 and 56.

21. SRO BRU 12/7/340.

NOTES

22. SRO BRU 2/2/262.
23. SRO ER 1/115/59.
24. CBB 21 February 1595.
25. CBB 5 July 1609.
26. Lewis Gilbert, a butcher by trade, grew quarrelsome while drinking in the house of Richard Waterman and, when Waterman's son, Thomas, tried to remove him, Gilbert drew his knife and stabbed him.
27. Ambrose Rookwood was one of the conspirators. He had rented Clopton House temporarily. Twelve Stratford men signed or made their marks on the inventory of his goods. SRO ER 1/1/55.
28. Dyer, 'Warwickshire Towns under the Tudors and Stuarts', pp. 122–33.
29. Martin, 'A Warwickshire Market Town in Adversity', pp. 28–38. In this article the values of Stratford probate inventories between 1578 and 1639 are set out as follows:

Date	Number	Total value	Average value
1578–99	65	£2,527	£38.17
1620–39	55	£3,848	£69.19

Similar calculations in this present study:

Date	Number	Total value	Average value
1578–99	66	£2,526	£38.27
1600–19	62	£3,461	£55.82
1620–39	51	£3,708	£72.71

Seven inventories made between 1570 and 1578 have not been included in this table. Eighteen inventories made after 1630 are included in the table but not in the study.

30. For the hardships endured by Stratford in the Civil War see Philip Tennant, *The Civil War in Stratford-upon-Avon: Conflict and Community in South Warwickshire 1642–1646*, Publications of the Shakespeare Birthplace Trust in association with Alan Sutton Publishing (Stroud, 1996), *passim*.

BIBLIOGRAPHY

Brinkworth, E.R.C. *Shakespeare and the Bawdy Court of Stratford*, Chichester, Phillimore, 1972

Clark, P. and Slack, P. *English Towns in Transition*, Oxford University Press, 1976

Dyer, Alan, 'Warwickshire Towns under the Tudors and Stuarts', *Warwickshire History*, Vol. III, No. 4, 1976/7

Furnivall, F.J. (ed.). *Harrison's Description of England in Shakspere's Youth: The Second and Third Books*, New Shakspere Society, Series VI, London, 1877

Halliwell, J.O. *A Dictionary of Archaic and Provincial Words*, 2 vols, 9th edn, London, 1878

——, (ed.). *An Inventory of the Furniture etc. of a Tavern in Stratford-upon-Avon taken in the time of Shakespeare*, ?1864. The book is undated but its contents were reprinted from *Collectanea Archaeologica: communications made to the British Archaeological Association*, Vol. 2, 1862–4

Harvey, Sir Paul, (ed.). *The Oxford Companion to English Literature*, 4th edn, revised by Dorothy Eagle, Oxford University Press, 1975

Hughes, Ann. 'Religion and Society in Stratford-upon-Avon 1619–1638', *Midland History*, Vol. XIX, 1994

Laslett, Peter. *The World We Have Lost – Further Explored*, Cambridge University Press, 1983

Martin, J.M. 'A Warwickshire Market Town in Adversity', *Midland History*, Vol. VII, 1982

Milward, Rosemary. *A Glossary of Household, Farming and Trade Terms from Probate Inventories*, Derbyshire Record Society Occasional Paper No. 1, 1986

Murray, J.A.H. (ed.). *A New English Dictionary on Historical Principles*, Oxford, Clarendon Press, 1888

Pollard, A.W. and Redgrave, G.R. *A Short-title Catalogue of Books printed in England, Scotland and Ireland 1475–1640*, 2nd edn, London, Bibliographical Society, 1986

Salzmann, L.F. (general ed.). *The Victoria County History of the County of Warwick*. Volume 3, *Barlichway Hundred*, local editor Philip Styles, 1945

INDEX OF NAMES

Note: Sixteenth- and seventeenth-century spelling was erratic. It is not unusual to find the same name written in several different ways in one document. The spellings given here are those used most often for that family or person in all documents in which they appear. Where a second spelling is given in brackets it is the one used in a quotation in the text. Women are indexed under both their maiden and married names where known.